The 5 Points of Power and Wisdom

A Guide to Intuitive Living

The 5 Points of Power and Wisdom

A Guide to Intuitive Living

Nicola Jayne

BOOKS

Winchester, UK
Washington, USA

First published by Sixth Books, 2013
Sixth Books is an imprint of John Hunt Publishing Ltd., Laurel House, Station Approach,
Alresford, Hants, SO24 9JH, UK
office1@jhpbooks.net
www.johnhuntpublishing.com
www.6th-books.com

For distributor details and how to order please visit the 'Ordering' section on our website.

Text copyright: Nicola Jayne 2012

ISBN: 978 1 78099 701 8

A CIP catalogue record for this book is available from the British Library.

Design: Stuart Davies

Printed and bound by CPI Group (UK) Ltd, Croydon, CR0 4YY

We operate a distinctive and ethical publishing philosophy in all
areas of our business, from our global network of authors to
production and worldwide distribution.

CONTENTS

To Love

Introduction

My name is Nicola Jayne. I am a naturally gifted psychic clairvoyant. I have worked with my gifts for many years helping to bring guidance, inspiration and peace of mind to many.

I have many clients who return to me time and time again, because they have found comfort and accuracy within my clairvoyance.

Many of the readings that I provide are through one to one private consultation. I also provide clairvoyant readings via e-mail and post available through my website. All of these methods provide strength, guidance, help and comfort to many.

I built the website myself and I feel very proud of my achievement. I'm often quite astounded since only a few years ago it seemed such an ordeal to collect my e-mails. It all seemed to click when it came to building the website; the process seemed to flow when I followed my intuition and it all came together. I am pleased with the website as it helps reach out to even more people.

I receive many e-mails on a daily basis, e-mails for psychic and paranormal advice, healing thoughts or simply prayer requests. With each e-mail I receive I feel privileged and humbled. I always do all I can to help.

Through the art of meditation I have opened my mind to connect to and channel guidance from my Spirit and Angel Guides. I am a practitioner of Tarot and Oracle cards. I am also a teacher of psychic and spiritual development and of Tarot tuition.

I am writing this book based upon the psychic and spiritual development courses that I have taught. I have divided this course book into two parts.

Part 1: The 5 Points of Power and Wisdom and how the impact of this guided philosophy can positively affect your life.

Part 2: Practical Exercise, Intuition and Psychic attunement, the keys to tap into your own psychic awareness.

I have been guided within my teachings and felt compelled to put pen to paper and share this wonderful knowledge. I provide the steps for personal empowerment, a springboard for expanding psychic awareness and intuition.

I base my psychic development courses on a guided philosophy called the 5 Points of Power and Wisdom. These 5 Points help bring personal power, wisdom and enlightenment towards a personal journey of psychic and spiritual development and understanding.

The feedback that I have received from students attending the courses has been magnificent; I thank my Spirit Guides for their wonderful guidance. My brightest wishes are that this book goes further and helps many, many more find and ignite that inner light that dwells within us all.

The 5 Points of Power and Wisdom

1. LOVE
2. BELIEF
3. GRATITUDE
4. FORGIVENESS
5. SELF-CONFIDENCE *This is my guidance.*
Now that I know this I am ready to Progress.
I am ready to accept the concept of these words and the
significance they will have on my life.

**We don't receive wisdom; we must discover it for ourselves
after a journey that no one can take for us or spare us.
– Marcel Proust (1871–1922)**

The 5 Points of Wisdom are simple steps of guidance for those seeking personal power and enlightenment. Like a pyramid the 5 Points of Power and Wisdom are a wonderful philosophy and deserve exploration. They serve to bring new heights of inner peace, power and fulfilment. These are the steps to the higher self and a higher state of conscious living. They will become a major landmark within your life. Take these steps today and seek a better life. You may have been looking for answers, but it may surprise you to know the answers have been there all of the time, within you, at the depths of your being. Now we can uncover these mysteries together.

Take the first steps on your personal path to inner empowerment, love, light, peace and inspiration. Let me illuminate your path every step of the way. I bring you love, joy, happiness, change and growth. Embrace these changes and also these challenges and let these 5 Points of Power and Wisdom impact your life as they have with mine and bring a new found sense of direction, happiness and abundance.

By following the 5 points you will feel a greater under-standing for yourself and others, and feel a deeper connection of love and empathy. It is when we have made that inner connection with ourselves that we can progress in mindful connectivity of intuitive living and psychic awareness.

I am happy that I can help those who are seeking guidance, inspiration and direction in their lives.
– Nicola Jayne

The Journey

I have always been aware of feeling 'special' and from a very young age I have always found comfort in forces outside our immediate physicality. I have found that from the very first few seconds of life, taking those first breaths of alien air, the midwife smacking my crinkly red baby's bottom to jolt those first gasps and screams. The trauma of life had begun. My foot was turned the opposite way around, and had to be broken and reset in plaster. I was this small baby with this great big white plaster of Paris cast on my foot and leg. It would seem even in those first days and weeks I was different, I was the odd one out of the babies in the hospital nursery.

This feeling would remain with me, throughout my life, that feeling of not quite fitting in, the feeling of being different.

As I grew, I became aware of an 'imaginary friend' or 'Spirit Guide'. Scientists speculate that imaginary friends are just that, a figment of the 'imagination', only existing in the mind. Spiritualists on the other hand would regard such phenomena as 'spirit friend' or 'spirit guide'.

Julie, who I regard as my spirit friend, was with me often, while playing in the garden, at tea time, at bath time and at bedtime. I would always insist my mum put dinner out for Julie too. She was even there when I set fire to the hearth rug. Back then, we lived with my Nana and Granddad Vin. It was a coal fire and I had observed the lighting of the fire with newspapers. I was just a toddler, and I had watched and learned. Sticking the newspaper into the fire it had quickly caught fire; I had become scared and dropped the flaming paper on to the rug causing it to set fire. Julie encouraged me to climb on to the sofa and quickly got me out of harm's way. Julie was very real to me. I believe she was a Spirit Guide. Here to help me, to protect me, to help me settle in to my new surroundings.

Growing up I was aware of a 'presence' around me. I refer to this as like being in my own fairy-tale land, as nobody could ever understand me, or believe me. They simply couldn't see what I could see. My family and close family friends would refer to me as being strange or the gatekeeper to Fantasy Island. In the end I kept quiet, keeping my visions and intuitions to myself.

Yes, I could see things that supposedly weren't there. My lights were switched on in the night, and so was my radio. There was a man that sometimes came and smiled at me from the corner of my room; later I found that this was my Granddad who had died years before I was born.

The apparition of a nurse who came to visit me one night while away on a school trip, just seeming to appear, floating in through the door, a transparent, bluish haze. I had broken my arm earlier that day, and lay awake in discomfort and feeling homesick. There she appeared through the closed door, dressed in old-fashioned clothing from what would seem the 18th century.

Then there were the dreams, the lucid dreams. I would wake shaken with these thoughts and real life panic and know something dreadful was going to happen.

I've always felt advanced for my years. I've always felt a strange knowing and an inkling of events yet to come.

The drowning dream, I would wake coughing and spluttering trying to catch my breath. I now know that Spirit was trying to warn me of what was yet to happen. Could they stop this predator, or were they meant to anyway? I do know that on that night while I was taking my Sunday night bath for school, and that predator came stalking for his prey, he stole my innocence and left me choking. Over the years I have worked through these acts of abuse and hold no grudges. I have released the past and forgave. I only feel thanks for every experience because without them I wouldn't be who I am today.

I dreamt of my friend Jane stood burning, flames engulfing her. I recall waking in a pool of sweat, wet through. I couldn't shake these dreams from my head of the flames roaring around Jane's feet.

One Friday evening, Jane had come to stay with her Auntie Margaret who lived in my street. We had been playing at my home very well with my toys, my mother had given us some chocolate cake and milk and all was well. Jane was happy and my mum and I got the impression that she liked coming to visit. After our cake we both went to visit her auntie in the flats nearby. I didn't like it there, it was pokey and stuffy. Her Auntie was a real large woman with psoriasis all up her arms and legs; there's nothing wrong with this, but to a nine year old I was convinced she was plagued or something. She always wore a smock-like dress, showing off her large psoriasis-covered arms and legs. Never the less she was a friendly woman. The flat was quite bare, and always smelled of stale tobacco and the dog that sat and scratched all the while. Jane's uncle would sit in his chair and never move. He wouldn't even move his head, focused on the TV, never uttering a word. Greased back hair with a roll-up in his mouth.

Jane stood chatting cheerfully about the chocolate cake she had just devoured as she stood in front of the fire. An electric fire with red bars hot and blazing. She was swaying side to side, happy and full of glee.

I noticed her blue floral print nylon skirt sway close to the fire, and in an instant I saw my dream, déjà-vu. It seemed within that same second Jane was ablaze.

Standing there screaming as fire tore up her legs, it happened so quickly; the nylon skirt melted to her legs and she was engulfed. The screaming was so intense and so horrifying it stayed with me for many years later.

I was surprised when Jane's uncle moved the quickest. Knocking Jane to the floor and rolling her up in the rug that she had stood upon. I stood rooted to the spot, shocked to my very core. I'm not sure how long it took for Margaret's voice to come filtering through to my consciousness, "Nicola! Nicola!"

The sound of her voice was like cold water being thrown into my face to rouse me from the shock I was slipping into. "Call the Police!" I ran home to have my mum phone the police. Not everyone had a telephone in those days. Of course at first they thought it was all in my imagination!

But after realizing that I was shaking and very upset they quickly acted. I never saw Jane again, and her Aunt and Uncle moved soon after the accident, but I did hear that after a long period of recovery she was able to walk again.

I felt very guilty for what had happened to Jane. I felt like it was somehow my fault because I had dreamt about it. I wasn't sure how to cope with my emotions about this. Why would I dream such things, especially if I could not help to make things better?

Now, when I have those moments of déjà-vu, which I often do, I realize it is the universe letting me know I am on the right path.

I found I became very secretive about everything. It no longer felt good to have this fairy-tale world around me; nobody believed anything I said. I began to tell lies about things that were really happening because nobody would believe me. I was tagged as being 'Queer'; I just grew distant and started blocking everything out.

As I got older and life tainted me, I began to lose touch with my spirit friends, and with my visions, until it all became a distant memory. My life was tough, and I found I had many hurdles to climb.

My childhood had been tainted with abuse, and this had only added to the way I had withdrawn, the feeling of being helpless; I wasn't able to confide in anyone. Who would believe me anyway?

Although looking back I now know it was essential for me to experience pain and joy, suffering and salvation, distrust and truth.

It was when the tides of life had come crashing against my sides leaving me truly vulnerable that Spirit showed up again. It was time to find my calling.

My life was very turbulent. I had suffered an abusive childhood, and walked into a relationship that was aggressive and violent. I had become self-abusive and self-destructive. Hope was just a word without any real meaning. I could not seem to break the cycle I had become trapped in.

One evening I was at home with my family eating our evening meal and the phone rang; we left it to go to voicemail. The voice on the machine was a voice from the past; it was one of my abusers.

It was such chilling moment; he had my phone number, and did he have my address? The sound of his voice and the threat and fear that this brought to me sent me into such shock and panic. I went upstairs and saw my daughter who was about the same age as I had been then, ten or eleven. I walked into the bedroom and my body collapsed into a state of panic, I couldn't breathe, and my limbs were shaking.

I was having terrible flashbacks and nightmares of the abuse I had suffered in my childhood. My anxiety was through the roof, I was literally a nervous wreck. I couldn't eat, sleep or go out. I stayed in my room because I felt so ill. I sought medical help and was told I was suffering with post-traumatic stress and anxiety. I'd just had a nervous breakdown. I was given medication to help me sleep and alleviate the symptoms.

A couple of weeks later I was upstairs cleaning up and the phone rang; it was him. He wanted to see me. He had missed me. I couldn't take it anymore. I put on my jeans and shoes, packed a bag, and took myself off on the train to Liverpool, some two and a half hours away.

When I arrived at the station I called him to come and meet me. We went for a drink at one of the bars in Liverpool Lime Street Station. I told him not to call my home again and to stay away. I told him that what he had done was wrong.

I guess I was there looking for an apology, but it never came. He wasn't remorseful at all. He told me it was our little secret and that I was still his girl. He saw it had been his place to give me love because he felt my mum didn't love me or give me any attention. He felt it had been his place to do this, and it was not wrong, and that 'I' had allowed myself to become a victim. He also told me that he had an axe strapped to his leg, and tried to persuade me to leave with him.

When I looked at him, I saw nothing but a broken man; I pitied him. An alcoholic, a criminal, he had nothing good in his life. He couldn't even see that he had done anything wrong to me, a child all those years ago.

I kept an eye on the time. I knew what time the next train was leaving. I got up to leave, and made a hasty getaway.

In the days and weeks following I began to feel much better about myself. I began to build my life. No, I did not get the apology that I was hoping for, but I forgave him anyway. I released my past. He was not worth being angry over. I realized that he was a very angry person. He was heavily burdened, and was carrying enough weight for both of us. What he had done was his weight to carry and not mine. This was his karma! I heard that a few days after my visit he had robbed a bank and was caught. He was later charged with armed robbery and was sentenced to twelve years.

I came to realize I had to forgive the others too and then finally myself; I realized I could be free from the past. I was then able to move forward much more positively than I have ever done before. For the first time I was able to set myself realistic goals and see new and exciting possibilities. I felt optimistic.

In Tarot I really found my calling and a channel for my intuition and psychic visions. It was like once I accepted the help I was given from above, everything was really natural. It was not like learning, it was like revisiting. The knowledge seemed easily gained.

Through meditation I have learned to centre myself, to connect and find inner peace and calm. I have been able to deepen my perceptions and wisdom. I have made connections with Spirit Guides and gathered a wealth of universal knowledge.

Through Tarot and other psychic exercise I learned how to become a really bright channel, sharpening my intuition and senses.

My journey has been beautiful, challenging, healing, transforming, inspiring and enlightening.

I have shed my past, like a butterfly emerging from a cocoon, finding light, beauty and love.

Most importantly, I have learned that nothing is impossible, there are no limitations.

There is a place within you where there is perfect peace.
There is a place within you where nothing is impossible.
– *A Course in Miracles*

Part 1

The Philosophy

Like attracts like.
Whatever the conscious mind thinks and believes the subconscious identically creates.
– Brian Adams, *How to Succeed*

Love

Every moment is made glorious by the light of love.
– Rumi

On my journey I have learned that only love is real. A true mystic will find a way to discover the truth and most loving outcome in any situation. Learning to find deeper ways and new depths to the being is the path to enlightenment.

Take a moment to imagine a life without love. Just imagine a situation or a time when you were in a place when you felt totally abandoned by the emotion of love. Take a moment to think about this. If your response is anything like mine then you will wince at such a memory; it is not a good thought process to think about or to imagine being without love. Because being in the absence of love is an unnatural process. If love did not exist then there simply would be no life.

I was once recommended a book by a very wise lady, she also told me I had a lot to give, I would help others, write a book and that I was deeply spiritual and psychic. This lady later became my friend in life, Maggie Sparke, a gifted Clairvoyant and Teacher. The wisdom and input that she has given me throughout my life has been priceless, and I love her dearly.

The book she recommended was *A Return to Love: Reflections on the Principles of a "Course in Miracles"* by Marianne Williamson. This book was the turning point for me; it really changed my perceptions.

I will not pretend to be a scholar of *A Course in Miracles* because I am not, although I have studied a little, just as much as I have studied Christianity, Kabbalah, Mysticism, Spiritualism, and other practices; I take what I feel I need to learn, disregarding the rest and move on. I feel there's only so much you can learn in one place, learning comes from experience, experience comes from living, growing and loving.

I was brought up as a Christian, and attended Church of England schools and church. My mum was approached by the Mormon Missionaries and we attended the church of the Latter-day Saints. I was baptized a Mormon when I was eight. I was fortunate enough to have had a fair and good experience of religion. There was a family who lived in our street who were Jehovah's Witnesses and they came to the house selling *The Watchtower Magazine*, a publication from the church of Jehovah's Witnesses.

I raised questions about this religion also; my young mind tried to grasp as much as it could about the many different ideas and concepts about God and Religion. The only conclusive idea I came to was Faith and Love were at the core of them all.

The idea of God, Jesus and the Holy Spirit seemed both mysterious and comforting to me. The Mormon missionaries had played a large role in my early learning. The brothers and sisters of the church would often be present at my home, teaching us stories from the bible and the book of Mormon.

I was once told by one of the kind brothers that, if I ever felt alone or afraid, then I should pray and ask for the presence of the Holy Spirit to be with me, and then I would be provided with comfort and company. The next time I felt fear and loneliness, I prayed for the presence of the Holy Spirit to come to me, and I swear I felt a presence with me, a strange comfort.

The Mormons also offered life learning skills that I have never forgotten, that I have taught to my children now. For example it was under these circumstances that I was taught the value of 'Family Home Evening'. This was one of the core values and I have adopted this as one of my own family values.

One night a week was to be set aside to be spent with your family, a family meal, a movie or games. Family time is important to me; I give my time only to my family here, it's all about strengthening bonds of love, especially as families grow and children become older.

As children grow into teenagers and young adults, their bodies and minds go through many changes. They become confused, angry and emotional as they try to make sense of their own identities. Because these adolescents are experiencing various strong cognitive and physical changes, for the first time in their lives they may start to view their friends, their peer group, as more important and influential than their parents or guardians. Because of peer pressure, they may sometimes indulge in activities not deemed socially acceptable.

To quote the respected Irish-born author, James 'Herbie' Brennan, the author of many esoteric books including *Astral Doorways* and also children's science fiction:

If there is one word to describe adolescence, that word is confusion. And when confusion is strongly felt it can easily impinge on your basic self-image. It's a sorry picture: small... help-less... powerless... dirty... confused – and in particular bad cases, unloved and unwanted as well.

When we are growing our minds are sensitive and easily open to suggestion, we are at times easily led. It can be the harsh criticism of others that builds our perception of our self. If we don't have a strong support, a strong sense of identity and self-confidence, that self-image will stay with us for a long time.

The home is an important aspect of adolescent psychology. Home environment and family have a substantial impact on the developing minds of teenagers. In the search for a unique social identity for themselves, adolescents are frequently confused about what is 'right' and what is 'wrong'. It is now that family structure, boundaries and routine play an important part in the lives and minds of the growing children in the family. The adolescents within the family are so full of questions and doubts about themselves, constantly fearing rejection from their peers; it is at home that we provide a source of comfort, warmth, love, acceptance and understanding. It is on 'Family Home Evening' that we all find our bonds again.

My own daughter has suffered such an emotional rollercoaster ride. It really has not been fun for all involved; but despite the ups and downs, I have always felt it was most important to show her how much she is loved, and let her know the meaning of a good home.

The Family that eats together stays together.
– Proverb

Within my own personal practice and ceremonies I do tend to stick with my Christian values and background, especially within prayer – "Dear God and the Angels, Jesus Christ and the Holy Spirit, please show me the love that is within me."

This practice differs with each person; each person has their own individual beliefs. I feel at this time it is important to grasp that there is one almighty force, one holy presence and that presence is Love.

Despite my religious background, I can honestly say I do not believe in religion now. This does not make me believe any less, I just believe in free thinking values! I believe that religion limits our thinking, or our beliefs, when really there are no limits on our thinking. God is limitless, love is limitless, love is effortless.

There is one thing all of the religious structures do have in common and that is Love. Love it would seem is at the foundation of them all.

To quote from *A Course in Miracles*, **"Perfect Love casts out fear."**

I never knew love or self-love in particular could be so hard, but once I found the strength in love and I found the beauty it had to offer me I knew I had found God's salvation. If I can love myself then I can love others too, because to treat myself with anything other than love is to do the same to my fellow man.

I felt trapped in an abusive cycle and this seemed hard to break. I was mixed up in a world that was filled with neglect, poverty, fear, hate, crime, anger and violence. I grew into my adult years not knowing anything else. It was a mere game of survival. I didn't think myself worthy of love.

I wasn't worth it!

Was I?

It is when we take a few moments to sit and think about how perfect we really are, what a wonderful creation! What a wonder, these eyes that allow me to see such beauty. My ears that enable me to hear my children's laughter, my nose, my mouth, my legs so that I can walk and my hands with which I write. My brain, this super computer transmitting every detail, my likes, my dislikes, my emotions are carried to the body, through 'Mind, Body' connection. The brain emits chemicals causing our bodies to respond accordingly. Thoughts cause emotional responses.

For example, the emotion of fear is related to adrenaline. If no feeling of fear exists there is no adrenaline and the same applies in reverse, no adrenaline, no fear. If we think positive thoughts about ourselves, and use positive visualization we produce positive emotions that manifest into positive physical sensations in the body.

The hypothalamus, the emotional centre of the brain, transforms emotions into physical response. The receptor of Neuropeptides, the hypothalamus controls the body's appetite, blood sugar levels, body temperature, adrenal and pituitary glands, heart, lung, digestive and circulatory systems.

Neuropeptides, the chemical messenger hormones, carry emotions back and forth between the mind and body. They link perception in the brain to the body via organs, hormones and cellular activity. Neuropeptides influence every major section of the immune system, so the body and mind do work together as one unit.

Give Love, Gather Love
– Proverb

Wherever a thought goes there is a body chemical reaction. Science tells us this is how the body transmutes using chemicals, as nature intended, as we were created. If I changed my thought pattern then my body would react, causing a chemical reaction, because I had believed. My mind and body are working together.

So yes I was worth it. I was worthy of love. Love is already programmed within us. It was a matter of changing the way I viewed myself and my surroundings. It was about changing my perception.

It's a matter of taking the time to think about how beautiful you are, about how much good is contained within; it is magical. Let the love grow for yourself and know that you are a wonderful person, and yes you are a loving, kind and caring being.

Remember with every decision that you make the feeling of Bliss tells you that you're home.
– Charles, Spirit Guide

Self-image is very important. For many years I was living a false reality, my self-image was false, made up of many barriers and walls all cemented together with layers of self-criticism, loathing, hurt, fear and despair. It was through finding these 5 Points of Power and Wisdom that I was able to reprogram my mind. Finding a better perspective I could see a positive future. I peeled away the layers of the false self and discovered my true self, the real me.

The real self is to know yourself, to love yourself, to discover yourself, to allow yourself to be who you wish to be. The real self is about accepting who you are, and knowing you deserve love and happiness. To know yourself is to give up all the negative barriers and attachments that stop you from succeeding, being and doing all that you want in life.

It matters not who you love, where you love, why you love, when you love, or how you love. It matters only that you love.
– John Lennon (1940–1980)

Know Thyself

All through the history of philosophy there has been an attempt to solve the mystery of life and the mystery of man. The earliest of these was the Vedanta of India, which said that nothing is greater than the attainment of the knowledge of the self.

The highest wisdom of the ancient Greeks was expressed in just two words, 'Know Thyself'. This precept was inscribed above the doors at the Temple of Apollo at Delphi.

Know Thyself, Take nothing in Excess.
– Socrates

We must always first look within to see without. Finding our centre, our true selves, and our higher selves is pivotal in our journey to success. When we come to know our true selves, our inner selves, we find a peaceful centre, we are true to ourselves, our needs, our likes and our dislikes. We are able to release the light of love within us and in doing so accept others, resulting in fulfilling and successful loving unions.

The Real You

Always be true to yourself and to your true feelings. Self-sacrifices always lead to resentment in the long run.

What do you like? How do you feel? What makes you happy? Find your Focus!

Knowing yourself is a journey to finding your higher self,

finding that centre, your inner calm, inner peace, balance and happiness. It is a journey of the spirit, of knowledge; the more you know yourself the better you will find your intuitive flow. The better you feel connected with yourself, the better you will feel connected to others.

Knowing others is wisdom, knowing yourself is Enlightenment.
– Lao Tzu

Learn and Grow

There is nothing more tragic to see than those who seem to repeat the same patterns over and over again, accumulating a world of chaos. Recognize failings, patterns and break these cycles. Do not fear changes, changes are an important part of our journey and often sent to aid our development in life. Inner happiness tells us we are on the right path.

Allow your intuition and senses to guide you. Whatever the situation, whatever part of your life, let that guidance be present. Trust, believe, feel, you are gifted, and that guidance is within you. Allow this to shine through to illuminate your true path in life.

The true self, the inner self is a feeling of being home, of complete contentment.

Know thyself, your temperaments, your cycles, your likes and your dislikes. Remember what works for one person does not work for everybody else. Do not allow yourself to be swayed by the opinions of others, and stand firm by your own. It is so important to live and experience life for yourself; choose your own path by following your feelings. Just because we are all connected does not mean we are not individuals.

I have witnessed those who are stuck in unhappy situations

because they took this or that person's advice. They feel stuck underneath somebody else's opinions and rules or because they are doing what society dictates. It is sometimes a case of, my family thought I should do this, so I did. When I ask, how about you? What do you think? The reply comes, I don't know. In the long run personal sacrifice only leads to unhappiness and an unfulfilled life.

I cannot imagine living some half of life. Never really knowing who I am, doing something based on the opinion of others. Or being too afraid to live my own life because it was not what others wanted. Not even trying because other people had told me that doing so would cause me to fail!

No matter what the situation the realization is that we come to rely on our comfort zone; no matter how grim that reality really is, any change is felt as a threat to that comfort and way of life. We see our foundations being shook at the core. It is hard to face a new reality, however, accepting and embracing changes is the start to releasing ourselves from an oppressive state of mind. We can open our mind to many new possibilities by realizing there are no limitations of the mind.

Exercise – Know Thyself

- Take a few moments to relax.
- Breathe deeply and allow yourself to relax.
- Relax deeply; allow your muscles to relax. Relax your arms, your legs and your shoulders. Breathe deeply, relax deeply, let go and unleash your imagination.
- Imagine another image of yourself standing in front of you. This is your inner self, the real-self. Your awesome self.
- Take a moment to feel happy about yourself. Look at the way your real-self stands, smiles, looks and feels. Look at how your real-self speaks and interacts with others.
- Notice how much self-love the real-self possesses.
- Now step inside the real-self and synthesize with your

inner self. Feel the happiness, love and joy that are contained here. See through your real-self's eyes; how good do you feel about yourself? You are confident and happy. You are a naturally loving being.

- Take a minute to feel totally happy with your real-self. Discover the true inner self. What are your goals and dreams?
- Notice how the true-self easily achieves set tasks. Notice the positive energy as your true-self is living their true life path and follows feelings and intuitions.
- Finish this exercise by taking a few moments to daydream about how it feels to live within your true-self. How do you feel? How do you look?

There is no limit on your learning because there is no limit on your mind.
– *A Course in Miracles*

What is Love?

Who would give a law to lovers? Love is unto itself a higher law.
– Boethius, *The Consolation of Philosophy*, AD 524

Many of the core religions that I have studied tell us that we are all extensions of God. God created us in his image, we are within him and he is within us. God is Love and we are the manifestations of that creative power. It is in our nature to feel love. Love is an effortless emotion. When we are feeling anything but love – fear, guilt, anger, hurt – we are pulling in the wrong direction. We are pulling away from home, our centre. Returning home to our centre within us, to the presence, is a feeling of love, joy, happiness and contentment.

To love others is to understand them.

Wisdom is clothed in Understanding
– Sefer Yetzirah, *The Book of Creation*

To identify others as you view yourself is to know them, love, care and empathize with them. Know that when your fellow man has walked the path of fear, it has taken him away from home. With wisdom and a loving non-judgmental approach we can help guide them and bring them back home to the presence of God, to the presence of Love.

When you meet anyone, remember it is a holy encounter.
As you see him, you will see yourself.
As you treat him, you will treat yourself.
As you think of him, you will think of yourself.
Never Forget this!
For in him you will find yourself or lose yourself.

– A Course in Miracles

When I conduct a Reading, I always remain mindful of the presence of the divine truth that I channel. I am an open channel for a higher wisdom, this light and energy comes from (God) The Great Universal Spirit, The Universal Energy, The Universal Mind, The Eternal Spirit.

I use the different phrases to differ from God here because although I use the name 'God', there are many names, or ways to describe God, the Omni-present. The presence of God is Omnipotent. God is a force, energy, universe, an All.

In certain Hebrew traditions God is referred to as Ain Sof – which means 'without end'. God is infinite, ultimate, and immeasurable – beyond our capability to fully understand.

However, it is within our ability to discover a wealth of knowledge about the Divine and Universal Mind with study, prayer and meditation. It is my belief that we are closest to God when we are at peace.

The scriptures are emphatic that there is one God – one Elohim.

Listen, O Israel, Yahweh your Elohim is One
– The Shema, Deuteronomy 6:4

Elohim is the Hebrew word, and considered the sacred word for God. Elohim is a gender-combined, plural word. The word Elohim is concurrently male and female, and simultaneously represents both unity and majestic plurality.

Elohim is a compound of the feminine singular Eloah with the masculine plural suffix -him. The word Elohim represents a majestic, awesome God that is beyond the ability of the human mind to fully comprehend. We can comprehend some of the attributes of Elohim, but the fullness of the Godhead is beyond our understanding.

Another Sacred and popular word for God is Aum or Om. It is said to originate in India and is widely used within Hinduism, Buddhism and also Jainism. It is thought that 'Amen' in Christianity and 'Amin' in Islam came from Aum, but lost its original pronunciation through history.

The syllable Aum is first described as an all-encompassing mystical entity. Today, in all Hindu art and all over India and Nepal, 'Aum' can be seen virtually everywhere, a common sign for Hinduism and its philosophy and theology.

At the beginning of creation, the divine, all-encompassing consciousness took the form of the first and original vibration manifesting as the sound 'OM'. Before creation began it was, 'Shunyakasha', 'the emptiness or the void'. Shunyakasha is more than nothingness, because everything existed in a latent state of potentiality. The vibration of 'OM' symbolizes the manifestation of God in form. 'OM' is the reflection of the absolute reality, it is said to be 'Adi Anadi', without beginning or the end and embracing all that exists. The mantra 'OM' is the name of God, the vibration of the Supreme.

In Hinduism, Om corresponds to the Crown Chakra and diamond white light. The Crown Chakra is often referred to as the 'God source'. This chakra when developed connects and heightens our awareness of spiritual connection, bringing a higher state of knowledge, enlightenment and bliss.

When we meditate on these sacred names, either repeatedly in our minds or by chanting like a mantra by name out loud, 'Om or Elohim', it is said to have a profound effect on our spiritual growth. It is said to bring a sense of love, inner peace, joy and enlightenment. Some say that the word Om and the word God translate to the word Love.

For every reading that I conduct I remain thankful to God for allowing me the opportunity to help; whether it is across the table or across the miles, I know the universe has sent this person to me for a reason. There are no coincidences, everything happens for a reason. I view every sitter with love, with empathy, with care, and always without judgment. I treat everyone as I would expect to be treated. I treat everyone like they are taking refuge within the arms of love. No matter of their colour, creed, morality, or economic standing.

I am often asked for guidance and assistance with love, relationships, and love life.

Below I have included an example from a returning client who had questions concerning love.

Dear Nicola Jayne

Hope you may remember me as you have done two readings for me in the past two years. I am coming back for the third time!

I hope all is well and you enjoyed the Summer Time.

I always like reading your e-mails and I feel happy when I do that. As some time has now passed since you've done the second reading for me I thought I would ask you to do a new reading for me, focusing on my love life and if you can say something about my future partner/husband. I feel really lonely and I haven't found any man who would be good for me. I feel that the whole thing is getting worse as the time is passing… and I am getting older maybe wiser, but in a sceptical way… Any tips would be much appreciated as I so would love to be with the person.

Many thanks

Kind regards

Mel x

I have taken the following section from Mel's e-mail reading.

You seem to have grown quickly for your years… You have this intelligence, brightness, and beauty about you and although I feel you do not always recognize it within yourself, it is there none the less… 'Don't judge yourself too harshly'!

You may have treated other people badly, but you have treated yourself the same way too! You must forgive yourself, and recognize that you have been trying to adapt and to make sense of your emotions and your circumstances! Often when we are hurting, we hurt others around us, this seems to be a natural defence mechanism, a kind of barrier to shield us, 'Hurt others before they hurt you'. Although it is now that time when you must recognize this aspect of your behaviour and also your personality, and you must allow those barriers to subside, because I am afraid with love comes emotion, and with emotion comes feelings, and when feelings are involved it leaves us open to vulnerabilities such as hurt, pain, challenges, but often when we meet the opposites, love is finding someone who challenges us, and has us question ourselves, our feelings and life!

Perfect does not exist! Mr Right does not exist! If ugly exists then we are all ugly! If beauty exists then we are all beautiful! We are all flawed, we all have our imperfections, our own ways, but in reality and in truth we are all beautiful creations.

All we can ever ask for in this world is that someone will come along and accept us for all that we are, our imperfections, flaws, weaknesses, and 'neurotic ways'! Forgive me, but isn't this Mr Right? The one who accepts us for all that we are past, present, and future, cellulite and all?

Don't be so quick to judge, love is a two-way street!

Although this section of the reading was intended for Mel, there is truth here for everyone.

The image of beauty that we seem to have is a media vision.

Male and female models on a large scale are air-brushed in fashion magazines, but yet cause such pressure to our young while growing and finding themselves. Adolescence is such a confusing time without this pressure from the media and celebrities to feel they need to look a certain way to feel accepted by the world at large.

I can go out shopping to the neighbouring town, sit and drink a cup of tea in the cafe and watch people. I have not spotted any models here, not that I recall, not in the ten years of living in the area. What I have witnessed is people, everyday people, just like you and me, functioning perfectly, living their lives. Tall, short, fat, thin, blonde, brunette, young, old, black and white, all living, doing the best they can and coexisting in unison. Isn't this what is important?

You try this for yourselves, observe the people around you. Remember this is not about judgment; this is about truth and reality.

Love is about acceptance, acceptance of oneself and the acceptance of others.

Lord, make me an instrument of your Peace! Where there is hatred let me sow Love...
– Prayer of St Francis

Love is an essence, an expression, an atmosphere, energy, an All. To be without Love is to be stagnant, lifeless, in pain. To be within Love is to be happy, energetic, vibrant, radiant and inspired.

People, animals, even plant life respond to the expression of Love. In fact it would seem all creatures great and small and what is considered all of god's creations respond to love.

We are taught that we are within God and God is within us. We are extensions of the Great Creation. So if God is Love, and we are extensions of this Great Creation, this great universal energy (God) then we are indeed Love. Our natural emotion and nature is to Love.

It is a scientific fact that plants will thrive when given better care and love. When spoken to and sung to, their flowers bloom rapidly and more vibrant. Their fruits are better tasting, sweeter and juicy. Prize vegetables are grown this way. Gardeners will leave radios playing in greenhouses as a form of companionship. While other plants that are given minimum care wilt and die.

Animals that are given better love are often more energetic, appearing healthy, glossy and more radiant. It is proven that a high majority of well-loved animals have better immune systems.

The 'Mind, Body' response.

Take cows, some farmers play music to their dairy cows at milking times and this drives a positive response because the cows produce more and a better standard of milk with this method.

It is true, the mind, the body, the whole responds to love.

The essence of love pervades everything. Words cannot express its depth or meaning. A universal sense bears witness to the divine fact.

God is Love and Love is God.

Love Conquers All.

Meditation

Meditation is essential in our practice of psychic and spiritual development. In our journey of understanding ourselves and our higher selves we must find inner peace, our centre. It is through meditation practice that I have discovered so much about myself and beyond. I have glimpsed inside the spiritual realm, spoke with Spirit Guides, Angel Guides and Ascended Masters. It is true we must look within to look out.

Meditation is deep thought, a serious continuous contemplation. The aim is to still the mind, reduce and deal with irrelevant thoughts so that a connection can be made with your higher self. Meditation does take practice to achieve but often brings wonderful results and it is worthwhile keeping it up.

The reasons for meditation are that of moving towards a quieter mind you are better able to attune to the higher self and the source of the spiritual energy.

Through practising meditation you can become more centred, balanced and harmonious at all levels of being; therefore, you become a clearer channel through which energies can freely flow.

In the meditative state the left side of the brain becomes subdued and the right side of the brain is allowed to register inspiration and this enables you to use the natural intuitive ability that all people have. When this happens you are able to reach out to the spiritual aspect of the self and to link more closely in harmony with the Universal Energy.

Spiritual understanding consequently grows with frequent meditation. The techniques of moving into meditation are numerous and must be set to suit the needs of the individual. They commonly include mental repetition of a prayer, mantra, word or phrase, listening to calm music, control of or listening to the breath, and also concentration on an object either visually or mentally.

Through Transcendental Meditation, the human brain can experience that level of intelligence which is an ocean of all knowledge, energy, intelligence, and bliss.
– Maharishi Mahesh Yogi

Through meditation the body is able to relax and function and therefore is in a better state.

Maharishi Mahesh Yogi was an Indian Guru who brought the Transcendental Meditation Movement to the West in the 1960s. He is most notable for influencing the Beatles and other celebrities at that time and is often referred to as 'The Beatles' Guru'. Transcendental Meditation is a form of Mantra Meditation. The technique involves the use of a sound or mantra and is practised for 15–20 minutes twice per day, while sitting comfortably with closed eyes.

Maharishi describes the technique:

Transcendental Meditation is a simple, natural program for the mind, a spontaneous, effortless march of the mind to its own unbounded essence. Through Transcendental Meditation, the mind unfolds its potential for unlimited awareness, transcendental awareness, Unity Consciousness – a lively field of all potential, where every possibility is naturally available to the conscious mind. The conscious mind becomes aware of its own unbounded dignity, its unbounded essence, and its infinite potential.

Transcendental Meditation provides a way for the conscious mind to fathom the whole range of its existence – active and silent, point and infinity. It is not a set of beliefs, a philosophy, a lifestyle, or a religion. It's an experience, a mental technique one practises every day for fifteen or twenty minutes.

The benefits of meditation are that you will normally receive direct experience of your calm unbounded inner self. When you connect with your inner self you will tap into a deep pool of energy. This energy will nourish and enhance all levels of your life whether physical, emotional, mental or spiritual. Life should now appear more effortless and the world will, according to your perception, be a more pleasant and enjoyable place, simply because you have connected with your inner self.

Regular meditation can help promote a sense of peace and calm and bring a sense of balance. If meditation occurs before sleep and especially with relaxing music this stimulates a state of relaxation and produces natural and healthy sleep.

Stress is a major problem in today's society. Up to 5 million people in the UK are 'very' or 'extremely' stressed through work. In the US 75% of the general population experiences at least "some stress" every two weeks.

Everyone reacts differently to stress and some people may have a higher threshold than others. Too much stress often leads to physical, mental and emotional problems.

In the UK, anxiety and depression are the most common mental health problems, and the majority of cases are caused by stress. Research by mental health charities also suggests that a quarter of the population will have a mental health problem at some point in their lives.

Stress affects different people in different ways and everyone has a different method of dealing with it.

The chemicals that are released by your body as a result of stress can build up over time and cause various mental and physical symptoms. These are listed below.

Mental Symptoms

- Anger
- Depression
- Anxiety
- Changes in behaviour
- Food cravings

- Lack of appetite
- Frequent crying
- Difficulty sleeping (mental)
- Feeling tired
- Difficulty concentrating

Physical Symptoms

- Chest pains
- Constipation or diarrhoea
- Cramps or muscle spasms
- Dizziness
- Fainting spells
- Nail biting
- Nervous twitches
- Pins and needles
- Feeling restless
- A tendency to sweat
- Sexual difficulties, such as loss of sexual desire
- Breathlessness
- Muscular aches
- Difficulty sleeping (physical)

If you have been experiencing some of these symptoms for a long period of time you can be at risk of developing high blood pressure which can lead to heart attacks and even stroke.

Stress can be a serious matter in this modern age. It is true that most seem to be running the rat race. Our seeming need to keep up with the constant pressure of the material world puts us under enormous strain. The biggest causes of stress are money matters, work and relationships. Whatever we have, why do we never feel we have enough?

By following a frequent meditation routine you can promote a sense of personal harmony and well-being, as well as spiritual gain and enlightenment. Meditation has so many benefits it is simply essential to life.

Recording and sharing experiences is helpful in assisting recall after meditation.

I recommend that you keep a Spiritual Diary and log your experiences.

Grounding is important when undertaking any work of this nature; it is important to make a good connection with the earth at the beginning and at the end of a session so that awareness can be expanded while the body is grounded. It is necessary to use a technique that will return the consciousness to a state compatible with everyday living when the meditation session is complete. This can include moving the feet, rubbing or clapping the hands, stretching the limbs, having a drink of water, or listening to some basic music. I recommend using the grounding techniques as described in the chapter **Psychic Protection**.

Development

It is assumed that having decided to follow this course you will be prepared to attain development or attunement. This development will consist of a number of factors, including spirituality, awareness, intuitiveness, psychic ability and sensitivity. It will embrace some, or all of these attributes.

Meditation is a major factor in your development and a meditative routine is essential to your progress and development. I recommend that 15–20 minutes a day is obtained.

I have included many meditative exercises for you to follow at intervals throughout the pages; I ask that you always enter meditation with good intentions. "If at first you don't succeed then try again."

Technique
Meditation and the Techniques explained

- Always wear loose fitting clothes for comfort and please make sure that you have visited the toilet beforehand. The aim is to rid yourself of as many distractions as possible.

- Use the grounding and protection techniques explained for you in the chapter titled **Psychic Protection**. When you have used this practice please begin meditation.

- Lay or Sit comfortably. Take three deep cleansing breaths. With each breath, deeply relax, letting go of your day.

- Realize at this time there is nowhere to go and nothing to do. There is nothing that needs your attention. For the next 15 – 20 minutes the world will survive without you. You are safe and entitled to take this time out. It is essential to your progress. Know this and allow yourself to relax.

- Allow your breathing to become steady. Relax your arms, relax your shoulders, and relax your legs. Let yourself just melt into a deep relaxation.

- At any time if you feel yourself experiencing mind chatter, draw your attention back to your shoulders and relax them again. You will find they have tensed up! Just breathe and relax.

- Take your time and view a door in your mind. This is your door, and when it is open, it lets in light. When you are ready, step through it.

- Step into the light, step into the sunlight. You are now on your first steps on to the 'Astral Plains', and on to higher levels of consciousness. There are many amazing experiences waiting to happen.

- Once you have stepped through the door, you will notice you are on a path. Walk down the path to a gate. Open the gate and walk through it.

- Once out of this gate we are presented with many different landscapes. Sometimes sandy beaches with a gentle lapping of the sea on the shore. Maybe we can swim in the ocean and visit the lost world of Atlantis.

- Often we may be presented with a beautiful meadow warmed by the sun. We may find a path and walk with the sun on our backs. Who will we meet? What will we see on our journey? What will we discover?

- At other times forests of azure, thick with possibilities. We may discover Totem Animals, Guides, and Spirit. We may find rivers and deep cleansing pools.
- Paths that are made of rainbows and caves that are made of crystals which seem to give us energy and healing.
- The truth is you have entered a land of endless possibilities. It is what we see, who we meet and the knowledge that we gather while we are here that counts. Travel well and with good intentions, and always document your journey.

Guided Meditation – Love

It is advisable when attempting meditation to wear loose fitting clothes for comfort and relaxation. First visit the toilet to take away any distractions. Place a glass of water at your side for the completion of this exercise. Play gentle and relaxing music to encourage a deeper state of relaxation.

- Sit or lay quietly and comfortably. Take in deep breaths and let your whole body deeply relax.
- Breathe in and out and relax deeply. Relax your arms, legs and your shoulders. With every breath let go and relax.
- With every exhale, think, "I am love."
- Repeat this until you feel yourself deeply relax, and you become aware of yourself feeling content. "I am Love."
- Allow yourself to SMILE a real big smile. Really feel happy now and pleased with yourself. Feel this, really, deep down at the pit of your stomach.
- Allow the sensation to sit there for a few moments; allow feelings of contentment and of happiness to expand throughout your body. Feel yourself smile at this beautiful sensation.
- Let yourself feel good about yourself. You are a marvel! A Wonderful Creation! You are so full of love!
- Reflect upon the love within you and allow this feeling to fill and expand throughout your entire body.
- Think of your kindness and loving acts, your goodness. The empathy and love you have for others and your loved ones. You are beautiful, allow yourself to know this, to feel this. You deserve love and happiness, this is your nature, feel your centre, feel at home!
- Allow your emotions to fill your body and your mind. This exercise can make you laugh and also cry.

- Let go of your emotions here; if you want to laugh, then laugh, if you want to cry, then cry. Release your emotions without fear, this is your time!
- Let go of the beauty that is contained within you, allow your emotions to rise to the surface. Remember love is a natural emotion.
- When you feel complete, open your eyes, you will feel refreshed, renewed, and feel a sense of completion.

This meditation exercise helps to reinforce your strength in love, and helps you to focus on all the good that is within; enjoy the feeling, release it and share it with others.

Belief

Men often become what they believe themselves to be. If I believe I cannot do something, it makes me incapable of doing it. But when I believe I can, then I acquire the ability to do it even if I didn't have it in the beginning.
– Mahatma Gandhi (1869–1948)

Visualization is not the same as Meditation even though many books link the two as being the same. Visualization is Active whereas Meditation is Passive. We can use visualization as a tool in just the same way as we can use meditation as a tool. Visualization is very powerful and one should not underestimate what can be achieved by using this tool correctly.

Visualization is a way of using the creative power of the mind to achieve a level of being, to move you to another place, to become someone or something different. When you use this mind power in such a way, the subconscious mind always responds.

Visualization is where we use our thoughts to create a scene or place, to create a set of activities, in which we take part. There are those people who say they find it impossible to use visualization; they are unable to create any form of image within their minds. This may be so initially, but as with all things, continued practice normally brings good results of progress.

If we stop for a moment and visualize, say our front door, take a moment. We use our door every day, to go to work, to take the children to school. We come home. We are pleased to be home, we feel weary and in need of putting our feet up with a hot drink for half an hour. We reach our front door, 'visualize'. We take out our door key, 'visualize', we put the key into the lock, 'visualize', we unlock the door, push down the handle and push open the door, 'visualize'. It is easy, you can visualize. With practice it becomes easier.

Visualization is a tool that can be used to help foster personal progress and growth. By providing positive pictures (creative imagery) and self-suggestion, visualization can change emotions that subsequently have a physical effect on the body.

Visualization puts your intention of what you want to work; the more specific the intention, the better the results.

Always **Believe** what we intend being accomplished. Once you are relaxed the next step is to actualize your visualization.

Think of or speak your intention out loud.

Positive Affirmations, Speak with intention.

Trust and Believe.

Close your eyes and imagine the process taking place.

Use creative imagery. See yourself practising clairvoyance, writing a book, driving a car, passing exams... whatever your goal see yourself doing this, feel yourself achieving this and the feeling you get from reaching your goal. Believe it is possible, and thank the universe for its arrival.

* Remember positive thought and feelings are essential to producing positive results.
* Negative thoughts and emotions lower the immune system, while positive emotions actually boost the immune system.

If you desire to have self-confidence and to be successful, then on a daily basis affirm, "I am Self Confident, I am Successful." I suggest using 'wall mantras'. I have positive affirmations stuck to the wall at the side of my bed. My personal wall mantras – "I am, I can, I will. To achieve is to take action."

Carry yourself with confidence and hold your head up high,

you have success and you have confidence, say thank you every day for your new found persona. Start to change your perception of yourself, believe it is possible to succeed. Soon your affirmations and positive output will have manifested your desire.

The universe always has a plan!

It's quantum physics, a mirror effect. What we give out always reflects back. In Wicca traditions, it is believed that what is given out comes back fourfold. In other words, we get back four times what we give out, whether good or bad!

Like Attracts Like

I always teach this theory, 'like attracts like'. While teaching development classes I always get asked, "Will I attract bad spirit, or negative energy, will bad things happen"?

The universe works with energy, we are energy, and energy cannot be destroyed, it is a continuum. Energy only changes form. When the body perishes, the energy that once powered the physical frame continues to exist.

So the energy that we give out must be positive to attract a positive energy back to us.

I always teach that when we are mindful of others, when we are good, honest, caring, when we live our lives filled with good intentions then it is this energy that will always find us.

To manifest good energy into our lives, we must, therefore, radiate good energy signals.

Thoughts Make Things.
– Ernest Holmes (1887–1960)

Ernest Holmes founded the worldwide Religious Science movement and was a uniquely gifted scholar with a vast knowledge of the world's spiritual philosophies; he is recognized as a twentieth century sage. In his book *The Science of Mind* he speaks about 'The One Great Law of All Life':

Thoughts of sickness can make a man sick, and thoughts of health and perfection can heal him. This law will work for him to the fullest extent of his belief in and understanding of it.

If we are to tell ourselves often that we feel ill then we only make our symptoms worse, lying down, slumping, feeling lethargic and stagnation. However, if we focus on the belief that we are fit and well, staying positive, bright, happy and hopeful then the chances of recovery happen quicker.

I read about a lady who had been diagnosed with breast cancer, however, she refused to give in to such illness. She continued with the belief that she would recover, and placed all her faith in God and Spirit. She stayed positive and focused. Laughing at every given opportunity and watching comedies on television with her husband to keep her spirits high. She kept this focus and belief. Remaining hopeful and optimistic that she would heal, she prayed every day for healing, and kept faith that all would be well. Much to the amazement to everybody, when she kept her appointment at the hospital for treatment all signs of tumour had disappeared.

To use such methods, as the Great Laws and the Laws of Attraction, it is firmly agreed by many scholars and teachers that BELIEF is the key.

To manifest a change in life and to usher in a positive change then we must believe that it is possible, we must believe, we must have faith that what we are asking for is granted, we are blessed. We have to ask and let go, it is out of our hands.

When I do this, I place everything into the hands of God. I view this like having a father whom I trust to give me all that I need. I don't worry, it will come when it is ready, I just wait for the signs, wait for it to show up, wait for some divine instruction. It is all down to faith.

Belief is essential to my work. I believe I am a channel, a clear channel for spirit connection. I believe that I am under the instruction of Spirit Guides and Teachers, and of Guardian Angels. I believe that I am here as a medium between this physical world and the world beyond the veil. If I didn't believe, if I didn't have that trust in the guidance that I was given, then I don't believe that I would be able to give successful, helpful, accurate guidance within my readings, because to doubt would be to disbelieve my own intuition. I have to have complete faith in my own abilities and the ability of the spirit world that is around me, because any other action would be to fail.

With recent widespread popularity in Cosmic Ordering and Laws of Attraction, with the bestselling books such as *The Secret* it would seem that there have been a new interest and a modern take on what is an ancient philosophy.

The **New Thought Movement** is a spiritual movement which developed in the United States during the late 19th century and emphasizes metaphysical beliefs and the effects of positive thinking, the law of attraction, healing, life force, creative visualization and personal power. It promotes the ideas that God is ubiquitous, spirit is the totality of all real things, true human selfhood is divine, divine thought is a force for good, all sickness originates in the mind, and 'right thinking' has a healing effect.

New Thought believes that God is "supreme, universal, and everlasting", that divinity dwells within each person and that all people are spiritual beings, and that "the highest spiritual principle loves one another unconditionally."

New Thought as a movement has no single origin, but was rather propelled along by a number of spiritual thinkers and philosophers and emerged through a variety of religious denominations and churches.

New Thought was also largely a movement of the printed word. The 1890s and the first decades of the 20th century saw an explosion of what would become known as self-help books.

In 1906, William Walker Atkinson (1862–1932) wrote and

published, *Thought Vibration or the Law of Attraction in the Thought World*. Atkinson was the editor of New Thought magazine and the author of more than 100 books, an assortment of religious, spiritual, and occult topics.

The following year, Elizabeth Towne, the editor of the *Nautilus Magazine*, a Journal of New Thought, published Bruce McClelland's book *Prosperity through Thought-Force*, in which he summarized the 'Law of Attraction' as a New Thought principle, stating:

You are what you think, not what you think you are.

It was many years ago that I sat at the kitchen table with my husband and my brother and stated that I wanted to work as a psychic clairvoyant. For many years I knew it had been my calling, but now I had surrendered, I allowed it to happen; I affirmed everyday: "I am psychic, I can read Tarot, I can do this, I believe, I believe"... until I had manifested my desire into a reality. Then it was a matter of affirming my confidence and my success. I had to believe in myself; if I didn't believe in me then how could I expect others to? The most important lesson I have learned is that there are no limitations. Success is where intention is. Anything that I want in life, I pray for, and then believe it will come. It really is a question of faith. I believe with all of my heart that I will receive what I need. I visualize what I have asked for and feel happy about this and always say thank you, because I know it is done.

It is important to let go of limitations. It is important to believe that anything is possible. There are no lack and no restrictions on the mind.

I started writing this book in January 2010. My faith has never left me; in fact it is as strong as ever. I use positive thought vibration often, and I use my wall mantras every day.

I have grown in confidence and have found a better balance

45

in my life. I have lost four and a half stones in weight. My frame is that of how I had visualized myself; I feel strong and healthy. I feel that I have really found my own sense of identity.

I have passed my driving test and I'm up and mobile, just as I had visualized and affirmed so many times.

I have separated from my husband. I finally found the strength and courage to become my own independent person.

I am happy, independent and confident.

Not that everything in life is plain sailing. There are still ups and downs. If there wasn't, how would we ever learn, grow or change? But knowing and having faith in the Great Spirit, in this Great Universal Energy that we are connected to, gives me strength and hope that all is good for the future. If I have achieved so much personal success in the space of just two years, then the possibilities are endless.

We are what we think. All that we are arises with our thoughts. With our thoughts, we make the world.
– Buddha

Gratitude

Gratitude is the fairest blossom which springs from the soul.
– Henry Ward Beecher

I always remember being a little girl in school and church; "let us give thanks and praise" was the term that was used as our heads would be bowed in a symbol of prayer.

I always heard the phrase "Thank God for that"; after some major or minor catastrophe in our lives, I say these words myself, but how many of us stop to think of the importance of these words.

Gratitude is one of the many gifts we must learn and never take for granted. 'Thanks' is never just a word or automatic response; it is in fact a powerful point of wisdom.

To be grateful and appreciative is a positive emotion or attitude in acknowledgment of a benefit that one has received or will receive.

For what I am about to receive to the lord I am truly thankful.

The experience of gratitude has historically been a focus of several world religions.

Let us give Thanks and Praise.

The study of Gratitude and the effects on the emotions have come under focus only in recent years with the 'Positive Psychology Movement'.

A large body of recent work has suggested that people who are more grateful have higher levels of well-being.

Grateful people are happier, less depressed, less stressed, and more satisfied with their lives and social relationships. Grateful people also have higher levels of control of their environments, personal growth, purpose in life and self-acceptance. Grateful people have more positive ways of coping with the difficulties they experience in life, being more likely to seek support from other people, growing from the experience and spending more time planning how to deal with the problem.

Having a positive attitude to life through being appreciative and grateful can cause a person to have a more positive outlook, feeling in good balance and good self-esteem. It also promotes good sleep and this seems to be because they think less negative and more positive thoughts just before going to sleep.

I give thanks day in and day out. Not only to those around me, but also on a spiritual level. I believe that Gratitude is a very important key to my success. I thank God for the love he brings into my life, I thank him for allowing me to realize my gifts, my talents, my potential, my strength and my self-confidence. I thank him for the energy, the wisdom, the guidance and the light that is channelled through me. I thank him for my Guardian Angels and my Spirit Guides that have been sent to help me in this lifetime. I thank him for each experience that comes my way, for each time I am given the opportunity to learn something new that helps me to evolve, to grow and to become spiritually stronger. I know every time I show my appreciation the universe smiles upon me, and then sends me more blessings to be thankful for.

I never thought that I would ever be grateful or thankful for many things. At certain points in my life when I was staring death in the face and sliding down into the darkness of my own destruction it would seem that I could never see the light of day, of hope or goodness.

I wanted nothing more than to numb the pain of existence. I was reckless, out of control, full of rage and hate. I was walking in the darkness, in the shadow of the ego. I was not happy, I had no love, and I certainly had no gratitude toward life.

She gave him her mind; Men came, gave and took, in silence she cried.
– "She Speaks in Triangles", Nicola Jayne (Poetry – *Dreams Unwind*)

I often still find it hard to comprehend how far this journey has taken me, and how valuable the 5 Points of Power and Wisdom have been in my life. I am no longer the girl I used to be. No addictions, no hate and anger. I found that I was able to forgive all wrongs in my life, I forgave those who trespassed against me, and I also forgave myself. I had to take responsibility for my own actions, for how I had treated myself and others.

For a long period of time I thought my life was never going to get any better. I just thought I would die an early death, and death would be a welcome release to the inner hurt and turmoil that I was feeling.

When my son was born I was 17. We lived in a one-room flat. I was so poor, I would drain the milk from the cereals to use again in the tea, and reuse the tea bags. My diet consisted of potatoes and bread. A sack of potatoes, 55lbs/25kg would cost around £5.49. I would buy a sack with my money and live off of this, usually eating chips, the big potatoes I would bake and eat jacket potatoes. The rest of the weekly staples were bread, tea bags, margarine, and milk. That was it. It was all about survival.

As my son grew into a toddler, I remember not having any money, and hearing his voice saying, "Mummy, I'm hungry." We were so poor that we would pretend to eat. Visualizing ice cream, sweets and chocolate and all kinds of delicious food in front of us and we would chew this imaginary food and then curl up and fall asleep together. It was this destitution and desolation that led me into a life of self-degradation.

Everything happens for a reason.

I had developed a sense of having no regard for myself. I often would go hungry to allow more food for my son. Producing food and a better life for him had become the focus of my life. My mind and life had already been tainted in my childhood at the hands of men. The further into the darkness I walked the more I became blinded and had lost my way. I started seeing and doing things that I am unable to comprehend now.

For a time I thought there was nothing that could save me. The goal of producing a better life was just an illusion, nothing was better. There was definitely more money and food, however, it had made its way into the home by illegal and immoral gain. I was fooling myself. I was trapped in a spiral of abuse, punishing myself for past hurt, pain and conflict. The only way I could survive was by burying my head in the sand and numbing life with drugs and drink. The birth of my daughter and the two months I spent sectioned in the psychiatric hospital only offered a brief pause to my destructive tendencies. Guilt drove me on, I had to give more, the more I gave, the more I saw, and the more pain endured. The drugs seemed to rob me of who I was, and started to take me from my home.

Where was I? Where had I been? Wandering endlessly, here and there, some floor here, some sofa there, in Scotland one day, Leeds, Sheffield, Doncaster, Bradford and London the next. I seemed to have lost my identity. I was so desperately unhappy. I remember my partner at that time picking me up from the side of the road; I had been missing for several days. With a fight, he managed to get me home.

I needed medical intervention to help me recover. I took myself to the doctor and threw myself at her mercy. Dr Alpin was very kind to me, telling me she knew this life wasn't for me, and that I had more to give and more to achieve. It was from here that my journey started to begin. I believe that I had really lived a harsh reality but also a vital one of self-discovery. I push myself to the limits, this is my personality. Whatever my pursuit I will put all of my effort in to it.

A few years later when I totally surrendered my life to God, I knew I had been stripped away to my very core, only this time I was ready to accept God and Spirit and also every lesson that was coming my way. I was ready to start again. I was ready to put the effort into my progress and into my life. I have no regrets.

Regrets can hold you back and can prevent the most wonderful things taking place in your lives.
– Proverb

I am often astounded when I look back and say I am grateful for it all, for every experience, every challenge and every hurdle. I am who I am and I wouldn't change a thing. I am thankful for the opportunities that I have been given to turn my life around, to learn, to grow, to become strong. I am truly grateful.

I am now more focused than I have ever been before, I am at peace, I am centred, I am loving, kind, caring, honest, friendly and approachable. I am calm, intuitive and creative. I am very different to the person I once was. I am now the woman that I want to be.

I thank God for love, peace and the many bright blessings that he has bestowed upon me.

O Lord, that lends me life, lend me a heart replete with thankfulness.
– William Shakespeare

Be truly thankful for every blessing that comes into your life, no matter how big or small. The more you practise gratitude the better you will feel within. Believe, have faith that for every blessing which you are thankful for another blessing is waiting to grace you.

Gratitude never deserts me. I know deep within my heart that I am truly looked after, and for that I am truly thankful.

Forgiveness

Forgiving is the path to liberation
– Buddha

Forgiveness is one of the most vital practices you will ever use on your spiritual journey. Life can be bumpy. In the hustle bustle of daily life, you will step on others' toes, say thoughtless things, and forget to recognize others' feelings. Others will do the same to you. Forgiveness is a given part of living life on a deeper spiritual level. Forgiveness allows you to strive to live at your best and know that when you fall short of that ideal, all will be forgiven. Forgiveness allows you to continue learning and loving fully.

Forgiveness is a creative act that changes us from prisoners of the past to liberated people at peace with our memories. It is not forgetfulness, but it involves accepting the promise that the future can be more than dwelling on memories of past injury.

If we could see the need to forgive in a built-up manifestation, then 3/4 of the entire population would be walking around with a dark cloud above their heads. The darker the cloud, the heavier the issue, the more the need is to forgive.

Sorry is just a simple word, but some find it hard to say, and if spoken without any real meaning then it creates no effect at all.

We all have some underlying issues, it is true, and we are all human. It is a natural response to get ticked off. It is also a natural response to forgive and move on, just letting the situation go, and live a harmonious life.

In my classes one of the weeks I set aside to have a forgiveness exercise. The class then is presented with the opportunity to release and forgive themselves and others who have hurt them, caused them pain and anger, or just simply got under their skin. A sacrificial fire is lit, and a list of names is burned while a mantra is spoken. Just declaring "I am willing to forgive" becomes a release in itself. Often this exercise brings such good and instant results like breathing fresh air and feeling like a heavy weight has been lifted, it's wonderful and cleansing.

I have come across the odd person who will not take part, claiming that they have nothing to forgive. It is usually this person who has the most to forgive.

I once had a friend, her children and mine played together so we shared this common interest. She had so many issues surrounding her, if I could see that Dark Cloud, it would have been a big black storm cloud for sure!

When she came to my home, she would be so very negative about everything and everyone. She never had a good word to say. She spoke badly about her past, present and future, about her family and friends. She even spoke badly about children and people who she had never met from the television. She held so many grudges against so many people, especially dwelling on past injury. I just became a sounding board to her. When she would leave, I would be left feeling drained of all energy and quite often I would cry.

This lady had to forgive her past, forgive the wrongs, let them go and move on with her life. Her negative mind set would not let her see that she was wrong about anything. She had nothing to forgive, everyone else was to blame, and she could not see any positive benefits to forgiveness.

I tried to influence my friend's life in a positive way. I would listen to all of her moans, gripes and abusive comments. In a way I was acting like a therapist. I would try to make positive suggestions and inputs to help change her thoughts and direction. This did not work and she thought that I was being mean to her, opposing her and attacking her. Why, because I did not agree with her, because I did not support her views, because I had a different opinion, because I made her question herself.

By making positive suggestions to help change her thoughts, I was challenging her comfort zone. Of course I was going to be viewed as an enemy. This lady had grown accustomed to her life and was now living a false sense of happiness. As long as everyone agreed with her, there was no problem.

Suffice to say a line was drawn under this friendship; I want to help people, but in life we can only help those who want to be helped. It is important to safeguard your own mind, energy and balance.

The simple act of forgiveness could have changed this poor woman's life. What was needed was a good downpour to brighten that cloud up again. Just learn to Forgive.

Instead of using forgiveness to aid her in her own personal development and growth she had allowed years of let-down and emotional rejection to build and build until she could no longer take any responsibility for her own actions. She had created her life based upon the theory: if you do not agree with me then you are against me, then if you are against me, then you are attacking me, so I am attacking you back. This woman had believed she had been wronged all of her life, and could not let anything go. When would this cycle be broken?

Forgive, and ye shall be forgiven
– Luke 6:37

There is no life in the past. You can never live in the present and create a new and exciting future for yourself if you remain stuck in the past.

Forgiveness is not about condoning behaviour, it is about learning to let a situation go.

Begin again. It is truly impossible to start anew and to make clear healthy life-giving choices until you have let go of past hurts, confusion and resentments.

Old wounds have a drawing power and pull our attention to them over and over, taking energy and hope from us, preventing us from starting again. Old wounds raise the fearful spectre of the same thing happening again in the future. For this reason it is so important to spend time understanding the true nature of forgiveness, and what it really entails.

To forgive means to 'give up', to 'let go'. It also means to restore oneself to basic goodness and health. When we forgive, we are willing to give up resentment, revenge and obsession. We are willing to restore faith not only in ourselves, but in life itself. The inability or unwillingness to do this causes harm in the one who is holding on to the anger.

Anger, hurt and un-forgiveness can be described as dis-ease to the spirit, to the mind, like a cancer that eats away at us, stopping us from living our lives to the full, and fulfilling our own destinies.

The weak can never forgive. Forgiveness is the attribute of the strong.
– Mahatma Gandhi

Forgiveness is the most important single process that brings peace to our soul and harmony to our life. All of us, at some point in our lives, have been hurt and wounded by the actions or words of another. Sometimes the grievances have been so great we thought, "No way, this I cannot forgive!"

Resentment and hostility can run so deep that forgiveness becomes very difficult. We feel we have a right to our indignation!

Forgiving is giving a spiritual pardon and helps with your own path to spiritual enlightenment.

Forgiveness is not something we have to do, but something we must allow to flow through us. When we step away from the consciousness of our human nature, and allow the light of truth and love to radiate through us, the light of universal consciousness to forgive through us, we can at that point just let go! I forgive you!

Once we have let go of our anger, our hurt, once we release this we can move on in life, we feel lighter at rest and so much better.

For example: You find your partner has been lying to you, you become angry, you are hurt and your temper gets the better of you. You both shout and speak words that are hurtful and the whole situation becomes even worse.

You spend the whole night in tears. The hurt, sadness and anger of this situation are all that you are left with. This feeling eventually subsides, until you are no longer an emotional wreck, just in a simmering rage. If you allow this situation to continue, the hurt will overwhelm you and you will become lost in a state of despair and sadness.

If you never repair the damage then you will eventually build a barrier around yourself to protect yourself from any future damage.

The truth is we are always presented with two choices at any given moment. We can choose to forgive and make peace with the situation. Remembering that forgiveness doesn't mean condoning someone's behaviour, but releasing and letting a situation go. We can choose to learn from the experience, by repairing faults, or by growing and becoming strong and independent. If we never forgive past hurts then the next lover that comes into your life you are more likely to judge on this past hurt. You will always be on the defensive, using attack as the best form of defence. Biting before you are bitten!

When things go wrong, in the beginning we are hurt, we argue; however, if we follow this with a peaceful resolution we talk, we forgive and we choose to let it go. We will come to realize that we are brought peace, our lives are harmonious, and we can resolve issues and move on. We become stronger and we are brought a sense of calm, a sense of well-being when we release our anger, when we forgive wrongs.

We realize nothing really matters at all.

The truth is it takes more time and energy focusing on staying angry and holding a grudge with someone than it does to forgive. I don't have the time for that, do you?

The concept of spiritual pardon sounds good, but how do we forgive people for acts that had a major impact on our lives?

As a person who experienced abuse during childhood, I understand the difficulty of forgiving people. On my journey of restoration, I've sought to forgive those who abused me in my childhood.

My life had been turned upside down, and I lived a very chaotic lifestyle. I found I spiralled forever downwards into a world of darkness and self-destruction. For many years I felt I would never find an escape from the cycle I was trapped in.

A number of years later, I was totally worn, on my knees and I had seemed to have been driven to the lowest ebb that I could possibly go with life. It was then that Spirit showed up again and my path took a new direction. Upon my path, my travels and my learning, forgiveness was one of the most important lessons I had to learn and that I had to practise. For once I had let go of the horrors of the past, once I had forgiven others and also myself, it was as if I could breathe again. Somehow the future became brighter and I had a better perspective, I could stop beating myself up, I found a new strength.

I now find it easy to forgive and let situations go. I can also view the past as relevant to my growth and to my spiritual progress in life. I feel that without the experiences, the hurdles, then I wouldn't have been presented with an opportunity to have grown spiritually, to learn; I feel fortunate enough that I have been presented with the opportunity to find a deeper depth to my being, to find a deeper sense of love and understanding.

A good Mystic is the seeker of spiritual love, light, wisdom and knowledge, through experience, intuition and insight. A Mystic will seek out the positive and loving path, discarding the negative in any situation, on his or her path to enlightenment.

Holding on to anger is like grasping a hot coal with the intent of throwing it at someone else; you are the one who gets burned.
– Buddha

Exercise – Forgiveness

Forgiveness is a major step towards spiritual growth and development. Forgiveness comes from the heart and not the mouth. When we forgive, we understand who we are and what our purpose is on earth. Forgiveness brings peace and harmony into our lives. It allows us to be free of any and all negative experiences. When we are free we are open to the experience of love, joy, happiness, success and peace. When we forgive, we learn. When we learn, we grow mentally, physically, and spiritually.

Only practise this exercise if you feel that you are ready within.

Think about those who have caused you upset, hurt, irritation or grievance. Those who you feel you need to forgive, situations of which you feel that you need to let go. In some cases this thought process doesn't take long and a whole stream of names or events jump straight in to your mind. If this happens, this usually means this needs releasing. Spend some time thinking this over and when you are ready write down the following:

I (Your name) am willing to release and forgive (Name) for the upset and hurt you have caused me.

Take this time to write about the episode and the way it has affected you; this is a good time to get rid of some unspent feelings.

– Each time you forgive repeat this mantra, either inward or outward or in written word.

I fully and freely forgive you.
I bless you and let you go.
I release you and release myself.
In love and in light,

I forgive you and release you to the Holy Spirit.
I am free to grow.
It is done, it is done, it is done.

You may feel the need to forgive yourself for actions that have caused others hurt or upset. Then write:

I am willing to release and forgive myself for the upset and hurt that I have caused (name).

Again take this time to write about the episode and the way it has affected you; this is a good way to release your feelings and gain a better perspective.

– Repeat this mantra – Again either inward, out loud, or in written words.

I release the burdens of the past,
I release you, and I release myself.
In love and in light,
I forgive myself and release this to the Holy Spirit.
I am free to grow
It is done, it is done, it is done.

Take this paper, and when you are ready burn it!

My recommendations are to have a ceremonial fire to release these burdens placing your letters on an open fire. Or light a white altar candle and burn your letters. As your Forgiveness letter burns, speak the following mantra out loud:

I release this, I forgive this, it is done, it is done, it is done.

The feeling is usually quite automatic. Almost like a weight has been lifted.

It is the act of intention that causes this shift in perception.

Note: Warning – always take special care when using fire! Use well ventilated rooms and take any necessary precautions to avoid hazard and danger!

Guided Meditation – Forgiveness

It is advisable to wear loose fitting clothes for comfort and relaxation when attempting meditation. First visit the toilet to take away any distractions. Place a glass of water at your side for the completion of this exercise. Play gentle and relaxing music to encourage a deeper state of relaxation.

- Sit or lay quietly and comfortably. Take in deep breaths and let your whole body deeply relax.
- Breathe in and out and relax deeply. Relax your arms, legs and your shoulders. With every breath let go and relax.
- Take deep breaths and allow yourself to relax.
- With every exhale meditate on the words: 'I forgive this, I release this...'
- Visualize a clear white light of beauty above you.
- This light has come to help take away any burdens. Watch this light as it grows, becoming brighter.
- The more you focus on this light, the brighter it becomes; it grows and starts to surrounds you.
- This light is beautiful and as it encompasses you, it makes you feel warm and comforted... I release this, I forgive this.
- Deeply relax with every breath.
- You now start to breathe in this white healing light; with every breath the light flows through you, right down into the pit of your stomach. The sensation will feel positive and light.
- The light stays there for as long as you need it. Feel it as it dissolves any old wounds.
- Stay focused on your breathing... I forgive this... I release this...
- You may feel many emotions, sadness, joy, love and

happiness. You may become overwhelmed by a mixture of emotions. Allow these emotions to leave you, this is a natural release.

- When you are ready to let go... repeat the words: "It is done, it is done, it is done."
- Butterflies will appear from the pit of your being, fluttering up out of your crown, many beautiful butterflies, watch as they disappear into the distance, every last one...
- What are their colours? What are your feelings?
- The nature of this meditation is for healing purposes; repeat whenever necessary.

Make a note of your experience in your spiritual diary.

Self-Confidence

Our deepest fear is not that we are inadequate. Our deepest fear is that we are powerful beyond measure. It is our light, not our darkness, that most frightens us.
– **Marianne Williamson,** *A Return to Love: Reflections on the Principles of a "Course in Miracles"*

Self-confidence is the belief in one's self and the belief in one's capabilities. I teach that you must establish self-belief and self-confidence in yourselves to follow tasks through. We live in a world full of cynics and sceptics who are all too willing to question our beliefs, our work and our principles. If we do not truly believe in ourselves, and have that self-confidence to stand firm in our position in life, then we will suffer the knocks that life brings. We must build a firm foundation for ourselves so that we don't fall at the first hurdle.

I do believe that every experience which we face in life is brought to us helping us to grow in strength and in knowledge, a lesson from the divine. It is our choice always, with 'right thinking', to learn from these lessons.

We have all been given free will here in this physical existence. We are able to choose our own destiny in life. I have learned that we are forever confronted by two choices, with two opportunities.

In truth we are all the same; skin, bones, muscles, limbs and organs we function the same. We are amazing creations. If you take a few moments to analyse the way our bodies work, we realize the magnificence.

Take the senses, and the sense of smell, and how we are able to identify different fragrances, how we react to each one and relate within seconds with feelings of like or dislike. Our eyes see and observe objects and people and within seconds the information that we have analysed washes through us without any effort at all, but within those seconds we have been able to digest so many details, colours, age, purpose and materials.

Exercise

- Comfortably sit in front of a mirror.
- Relax and allow yourself to feel comfortable in this moment.
- Gaze at yourself in the mirror. First allow your gaze to focus upon your eyes; look at the colour, are they blue, brown, maybe green? Take in the brilliance of this colour. Look at the shape and the beauty of your eyes. Think about how much your eyes have seen, how much beauty which is in the world that your eyes allow you to witness on a daily basis. A beautiful sunset or sunrise perhaps, the warmth of a friendly smile, butterflies, babies and children and the many wondrous and vibrant colours of flowers, trees and fruit of the earth.
- Examine your nose; breathe deeply now, in and out, with each breath feel truly cleansed. Whether you consider your nose to be large or small it is perfect. As you breathe in and out, recognize this.
- Place your attention on your mouth, the sensual mouth. We express many emotions here, anger, passion, love. It is with our mouths that we taste the many delights of the earth. From our mouths we now express our feelings to ourselves – "I am perfect in every way, I am a perfect creation, I am beautiful." Repeat like a mantra...
- "I am perfect in every way, I am a perfect creation, I am beautiful."
- We now turn our focus to the ears. Our ears allow us to hear the sound of children's laughter, the sound of a newborn baby's cry, the sound of music. It is also with our ears we hear spoken words. We realize in this moment, we

choose to listen to our mantra.

- "I am perfect in every way, I am a perfect creation, I am beautiful."
- You are beautiful! And the longer you gaze at your face, your hair, your feet, your body, you realize that all is as it should be, you are an amazing creation. Limbs and organs all functioning and working to keep us strong, healthy and alive. Recognize your beauty often.

To end this exercise, spend a few more moments repeating the mantra and allowing yourself to feel happy and beautiful within and without.

It is quite usual to feel silly at first. Sometimes others find this exercise difficult due to a poor self-esteem, but with constant effort this exercise becomes easier and more beneficial.

Have you ever had problems visiting the hairdresser? It is not uncommon for those with a low self-esteem to have problems with this. It isn't that people with a low self-esteem don't want to have good hair or even that they feel that they don't deserve to have their hair styled and cut. In fact a high percentage of people with self-esteem issues will make do with self-styling their own hair or won't bother altogether. The problem with visiting the hairdresser is the 'mirror'. The fact is you are faced with the true image of yourself. If you don't feel good about yourself, then one of the worst things that can happen is that you are forced to face your own reflection. Having a low self-esteem can quickly lead to issues with self-image and then this becomes a hard cycle to break.

So God Created Man in his own image, in the image of God created he him; Male and Female created he them.
– Genesis 1:2

Right Thinking

With right thinking we can create a world filled with success. It is about our perception. We have two paths at all times facing us. Path One is that of the Higher Self, and the second path that of the Ego. The first path is where we find our higher self, illuminated by light, love, of positive thinking, motivation, action and abundance. The second path is where the ego dwells in darkness of negative forces and influences, restriction, oppression, chaos, fear, anger and lack.

These two paths are the two polar opposites within life, the yin and yang, the good and the bad, the light and the dark, the male and the female force within each of us. It is the free will which we possess that we use to choose one of these destinies for ourselves. It is only with our change in thought and perception that we can change our path, our fate and our destiny at any time. I did. And I know you can too. It starts with a single thought, in a single moment, 'I am love'.

It is through this thought process that we build our self-confidence. Building self-confidence is essential to our progress. I have said many times, "If I don't believe in me, then how can I expect anyone else to?"

When we visualize goals for the future, when we see ourselves achieving all that we are hoping for, do we see ourselves as incompetent, shy, lacking or introverted? Of course not, quite the opposite. We see ourselves being strong, focused, determined and happy. It is this image we must focus on.

Some people are so afraid of failure that they will never try to succeed in the first place. We must try and break cycles that we have become used to. It is hard but often in childhood we may have been told, "You can't do this or that, you're no good at sports," and "you're like me too clumsy." "You're no good with numbers; it just doesn't run in the family." "You'll never learn to dance, two left feet."

Parents aren't perfect, and as all parents know parenting does not come with a manual, we all just do our best. We learn from our parents, and our parents have learned from their parents and so on…

Through no fault of their own, parents often contribute to self-esteem and self-confidence issues. Whatever it seemed to be that they told us, or actions we witnessed or were involved in while growing, a large percentage will blame parents and their childhood for their self-image today.

My father wasn't there for me! My family was poor! My mother didn't care! My parents never understood me! They never supported or encouraged me!

All of these statements reflect issues of abandonment, lack and neglect in adulthood. We grow feeling whatever we do, or whatever we have, is never enough. This simply isn't true. As we build our self-esteem and self-worth, we let go of our past using forgiveness and with positive thinking we come to realize that we are more than enough and we are definitely worth it.

We cannot live our lives living in a certain mind set forever more, based on blame, grudges, or what the opinion was way back in the day. We can turn our lives around at any moment.

It is that choice within each of us; it is that inner strength. We all have our own minds, and I ask you to change your thoughts now.

Instead of thinking, 'I can't', think 'I can'!

Many people live life blaming others for how their life has turned out, whether they are blaming their mother, father, classmates, teachers, employers or the government. They pin the blame on somebody else for their own failings.

It is essential to take control of your own life, take responsibility for your own actions. It is not about blaming yourself. It's about taking control, taking responsibility for your own life. We are not responsible for the hand we have been dealt in life, but it is in our hands and our control how we choose to play the hand that life has dealt us.

We can choose to take every obstacle as a sign that the whole world is against us, seeing any minor downfall as major failings. We may even use phrases such as, 'nothing ever goes right for me' or 'when it rains it pours'. Always expecting the next downfall, the next catastrophe, and why not, because life just always dumps on me! We may even think, 'I was never given a chance at school', and 'my employer hates me'. Your mind is set to fail. What we think is what we create for ourselves.

You can choose to play your hand with responsibility, care and control, by seeing any obstacle as a stepping stone and a learning curve. Adopting such sayings as: 'I will remember that lesson and learn from that', 'I won't repeat that mistake again' and 'I can achieve anything that I put my mind to'. You may look at life with positivity and self-belief adopting an attitude of self-worth. You find a positive energy flow, a get up and go feeling, and a successful attitude towards life. This right thinking happens when we start taking responsibility for our actions; this comes when we change our perceptions about ourselves and about life.

Whatever we focus on consistently we manifest into our lives. Power comes from concentrating your focus daily on positive manifestation and taking daily action to create positive changes within your life.

See every difficulty as a challenge, a stepping stone, and never be defeated by anything or anyone.

When you take responsibility for your life you gain personal power and wisdom. You begin making right choices and changes in every area of your life. You take control of your relationships, health, education, career and also your finances.

I left school and home at the age of fifteen; the circumstances around me at this age made my life hard and unbearable. I had no qualifications and I had no knowledge of life. Over the years I have learned to take control of my own life and destination. If I want to achieve something then I put my focus and intention into this and with strength and determination I achieve this for myself.

To help boost my own self-confidence I have taken an English course at a night school passing my GCSE at A* level. I wanted to take this course to help with my grammar, and written work. Also at night school I took a course in Art to help better my creative work. My other achievements include passing a course in Indian Head Massage and Spiritual Energy Healing, and becoming a Reiki Master. All of these achievements are personal to me; they were to aid my future and my personal growth. It is a very good feeling to realize that you can actualize your goals. When you start ticking off your achievements you are on your way to success.

It is about changing your mind set and reprogramming your mind.

I have always had an issue with my weight. The fact that in that sentence I have included the word 'issue' will always manifest an issue with my body and with my weight. I am in the process of changing my thought pattern about this; it is difficult, due to years of being told and of telling myself I have weight issues. I am determined to succeed!

My focus: 'I am healthy; I eat when I'm hungry and stop when I'm full, I will succeed'. My thought pattern has changed and with positive focus I will succeed.

I am now telling myself to listen to my body. What does my body want and need. I visualize myself at my ideal weight. How do I look? How do I feel? I am happy and I feel confident.

Since starting to write this book over two years ago, I have achieved this goal and have lost over 4 stones in weight and my dress size is at a size 10. I am very proud of this achievement. I am now how I visualized myself to be.

Changing your perceptions actually do work. With positive focus and belief, it is amazing what you can achieve.

My mother also has weight concerns; while growing up I remember she would always be on some diet here or there, losing weight and then gaining even more. I grew up in a home where the meals were large, and I was always encouraged to finish my meal, so I have always overeaten, eating even after I am full. We learn from what we have seen for ourselves.

I have now trained my mind and body to stop eating when I realize I am no longer hungry and also cut down on the size of portions I serve up. My little boy brought this cycle to my attention when he said to me, "Why do I need to keep eating when I'm full up"? Of course I was just practising what I had been taught, "Eat it all up. That's a good boy. There are starving kids in Africa you know!" I'm not trying to make my kid fat, my mum was not trying to make me fat, it's just a cycle, a learned tradition, although that doesn't make it right.

I can now take responsibility for my health, diet, and eating habits. I can now change this cycle by taking control and changing the way I think about it. With right thinking and positive focus I can manifest a positive reality and boost my self-esteem and confidence.

What is Self-Confidence?

Two main elements contribute to self-confidence: self-efficiency and self-esteem.

We gain a sense of **self-efficiency** when we see ourselves mastering skills and achieving goals. This self-efficiency comes from learning to achieve on our own in any chosen area of our lives, whether this may be study, work or developing a successful home and love life. This skill comes from learning that within you are strong, dependable and self-efficient.

We then gain greater confidence with **self-esteem**; this comes from achieving our goals and gaining results and allowing ourselves the recognition we deserve after attaining goals and noting our progression in life.

Always keep a spiritual diary. I have mentioned this several times throughout the chapters; I want to note here how important it is. I keep a diary and document my experiences, my goals and my achievements. I can then look back over my accomplishments and at times this can provide a much needed self-esteem boost, and refresh your vision and outlook.

I believe that self-confidence can be built using and following the 5 Points of Power and Wisdom. Positive Affirmations, Visualization and Meditation are among the many Mind Tools available to you within this Course. It is just as important to build self-confidence by setting and achieving goals, thereby building competence.

Using the exercises and meditations regularly you will discover your life changing and becoming forever more positive.

Success comes in cans, not can'ts.
– Proverb

Developing Self-Confidence

Self-confidence is an attitude which allows individuals to have positive yet realistic views of themselves and their situations. Self-confident people trust their own abilities, have a general sense of control in their lives, and believe that they will be able to do what they wish, plan, and expect. Having self-confidence does not mean that individuals will be able to do everything. Self-confident people have expectations that are realistic. Even when some of their expectations are not met, they continue to be positive and to accept themselves.

People who are not self-confident depend excessively on the approval of others in order to feel good about themselves. They tend to avoid taking risks because they fear failure. They generally do not expect to be successful. They often put themselves down and tend to discount or ignore compliments paid to them.

By contrast, self-confident people are willing to risk the disapproval of others because they generally trust their own abilities. They tend to accept themselves. They don't feel they have to conform in order to be accepted.

Strategies for Developing Confidence

- **Emphasize Strengths.** Give yourself credit for everything you try. By focusing on what you can do, you applaud yourself for efforts rather than emphasizing end products.
- **Take Risks.** Approach new experiences as opportunities to *learn* rather than occasions to win or lose. Doing so opens you up to new possibilities and can increase your sense of self-acceptance. Not doing so turns every possibility into an opportunity for failure, and inhibits personal growth. Life is a continuum of learning; even when situations don't seem to have gone as planned, you will have still gained valuable knowledge from that experience.
- **Use Self-Talk.** Use self-talk as an opportunity to counter harmful assumptions. For example, when you catch yourself expecting perfection, remind yourself that you can't do everything perfectly, that it's only possible to try to do things and to try to do them well. This allows you to accept yourself while still striving to improve. Remember, "Success is where intention is."
- **Self-Evaluate.** Learn to evaluate yourself independently. Doing so allows you to avoid the constant sense of turmoil that comes from relying exclusively on the opinions of others. Focusing internally on how you feel about your own behaviour, work, etc. will give you a stronger sense of self and will prevent you from giving your personal power away to others. Give yourself credit when recognizing good work or achievements.
- **Positive Affirmation.** Using positive affirmations is like mental engraving, the more you tell yourself something the

more you come to believe it. This is a focus for the mind, and helps with positive thinking and the building of self-confidence.

- **Positive Visualization.** Visualizing goals and their outcomes helps keep clear your intentions for the future. It helps you keep a clear focus. Set small attainable goals on your journey. Each time you achieve a small goal, keep a log of all of your achievements in your diary, and praise yourself accordingly. Depending on your self-esteem level the goals that you set for yourself may differ. For instance a walk through the park, a trip to the shops may be a huge achievement for someone suffering with very low self-esteem. By overcoming difficulties and accomplishing small goals upon your journey you build self-confidence and manifest personal power.

If along your journey using the 5 Points of Power and Wisdom you log experiences, achievements and goals in a spiritual diary, this will become like a landmark in your life. What a wonderful boost this will become when you look back and see what you have accomplished using all of these powerful mind tools.

The Concept of a Successful Man

Could we see the mentality of a successful man, we should find the imprint of successful man; we could find the imprint of success written in bold letters across the doorway of his consciousness. The successful man is sure of himself, sure of what he is doing, certain of the outcome of his undertakings. As much gathers more, as like attracts like, so success breeds greater success, and conviction is attended by certainty. The whole teaching of Jesus is to have faith and to believe. He placed a greater value on faith and belief than any individual who has ever taught spiritual truth. We are to believe in ourselves because we have first penetrated the invisible cause back of the real self. We are to have absolute faith in our work, because we have positive conviction of the inner power which enables us to do this work.

– Ernest Holmes (1887–1960), *The Science of the Mind*

I will end this chapter by sharing a family saying that has been passed down from generation to generation. When I was a child my mum would drive me crazy with this saying. I suppose because my young mind could not fully grasp the importance and the full meaning of the words. So as my old mum would say, **"There's no such word as can't."**

The Power of Intention

'Success is where intention is.'
I am intuitive, I am happy, I am confident, I am successful...

You can deepen your spiritual quality of intuition by using affirmations.

Affirmations remind you that actions follow intentions. When you set your intention to achieve a goal, you choose actions to reach your objective. Affirmations are like guideposts, keeping you on the path to achieving your intended resolutions.

Negative self-talk is like static feedback of the mind, limiting your connection with your inner wisdom. Affirmations readjust your inner dial of thoughts, aligning your intentions with your desired outcomes. When your thoughts reflect your divine potential, you pull from the well of Spirit to support and manifest your divine purpose. Buddhists call this 'Mindful Living', where you are conscious of your thoughts and the impact that your actions have upon yourself and others.

When you use affirmations, you remain true to your divine path by tapping into your spiritual mastery, intuition, love, inner wisdom, strength and forgiveness. Affirmations open you to these spiritual qualities that are already present within, strengthening your awareness of your spiritual power to create life-changing results.

Remember you are a channel, a bright channel for divine guidance, wisdom and love. As you further come to know this and understand this, your intuition grows stronger as the channel grows brighter.

The most important lesson I have learned while working with my Spirit Guides is 'There are no limitations.'

We only ever place limitations on our own minds and lives.

Can we recall a time, maybe when we were children, and we

told a lie. Maybe we told a huge but harmless lie to our play friends. This is not uncommon. Perhaps the lie was, "I'm going to have a huge birthday party with clowns and jelly and ice cream," and in reality you were having a friend over for tea. Or maybe after the summer holidays you returned to school and told of globetrotting somewhere exotic, perhaps Egypt, swimming with dolphins or Disneyland. When the reality was, you were visiting Grandma in the countryside. As children we innocently put so much thought and heart into the lie that we become a part of it, almost believing it to be true.

Whatever the lie, if we tell it often enough, and with all of our heart we come to believe it; it's as if it becomes a part of us, because it is what we desire.

Usually the lie is invented because we feel a sense of lack within. We all have this undeniable quality to want better for ourselves, and the truth is, we do deserve the best in life, and there should be absolutely nothing to stand in our way of succeeding. Remember, 'No Limitations'.

If we lack self-confidence, but need more, then in order to achieve this, we then dress up in smart shoes and clothes, we groom ourselves appropriately. We speak with conviction and truth, we tell ourselves: "I am confident, I am happy, I look good, I smell good, I will succeed." The more you do this, the more you become that confident person you are trying to be.

Believe, Affirm and Thank.
I am a Perfect Channel for Light, Energy, Love, Guidance and Wisdom – I am Intuitive!
I am Loving, Harmonious, Happy, Confident and Strong.
I am Caring and Kind. I give Love and I attract Love.

Life is an almighty force, a force to be reckoned with. If we don't challenge that force then we will never win through. Some of us choose to just give in, to just give up, allowing ourselves to be beaten, to be ground down, while others choose to keep fighting. With strength, determination, energy, intention and positive thought, you finally find you win through and somehow this almighty force has got behind you and is helping you to manifest your dreams and desires. You are no longer just ticking off the days, you are ticking of achievements. It all begins with the power of positive thought and intention.

Take action. Take control. Life doesn't just happen. You have to make it happen. Remember take control of the hand that you were dealt with. Never be afraid of change.

It all starts with the power of Intention.

Guardian Angel Affirmation

I channelled this affirmation from my Guardian Angel. I keep this affirmation close by me always and say these words frequently.

The words within the affirmation strengthen my belief and faith. Although I channelled this affirmation several years ago they really do keep in alignment with the 5 Points of Power and Wisdom.

This affirmation reminds me of what is truly important in my life.

I am happy and free of all desires.
I deserve happiness.
I deserve health.
I am loved and cherished by God and the Angels.
I am loving and kind to all that I meet.
I set good examples to my children and to those around me.
I deserve the best for myself and for my family.
With positive thinking and a loving, kind attitude to others abundance will find me.
Gratitude will never desert me.
I choose to forgive all wrongs in my life and move forward into a productive, loving, bright future.
By choosing to love today, I release all negative energy that surrounds me.
I only attract positive energy.
By choosing to love and forgive, I am choosing to be happy.

Part 2

Psychic Development in Practice

Never discourage anyone... who continually makes progress, no matter how slow.
– **Plato**

Intuition

I feel there are two people inside me – me and my intuition. If I go against her, she'll screw me every time, and if I follow her, we get along quite nicely.
– Kim Basinger

Every person is born with that inner sense we call 'intuition'. Intuition is what often steers us away from danger, or warns us of trouble ahead. Intuition is that gut feeling, that knowing, that certain feeling! Basic intuition once trusted can be developed into psychic ability.

What is Intuition?

Intuition begins with instinct, and is a universal gift to all living things. It is a unity of the six senses: feeling, seeing, hearing, smelling, tasting and sensing that is unimpaired by either time or space. Instinct enables living creatures to live, procreate and survive.

For example, at the time of the 2004 Tsunami a devastating 150,000 people were dead or missing and millions left homeless in 11 countries. However, few animals seemed to be caught off guard. Wild animals left their usual territories and breeding grounds and sought the safety of higher ground days before the tsunami struck. Domestic animals and zoo animals were reported to show strange behaviour, refusing to leave their homes or enclosures.

Is it because these animals are so untainted by worldly matters, so in tune with their instincts, that they could feel the vibration shift of the earth, and sense with their natural instinct and intuition that danger was coming?

Intuition is a knowing that something is so, even in the absence of objective evidence. The largest hurdle is learning to trust in your own instinct, your own feelings, and to develop that into your own psychic intuition.

- Intuition is receiving energy in the form of feelings or vibes that make you instinctively know something significant about the person, event, or place.
- You must never try to analyse your 'message'; take whatever you receive at face value. The more you question your message the more you seem to contaminate the experience. It's about Belief.
- You cannot force intuition to happen. You are an open channel. The more open you are, the brighter the channel, the louder the message.
- Ask and you shall receive.
- Six senses combined. Your intuition works this way. The messages can come in a variety of ways. Through feelings, thoughts, images, symbols, sounds and smells.

Hippocrates, the fifth century BC philosopher known as the father of medicine, wrote:

Intuition is the instinct of the earlier races, when cold reason had not as yet obscured man's inner vision... Its indications must never be disdained, for it is to instinct alone that we owe our first remedies.

When following the 5 Points of Power and Wisdom and the guidance that the course has to offer we begin to awaken our senses, awareness and our intuition.

We are all guided to each other, the universe is a mass calculated plan, there are no coincidences, everything happens for a reason. It is a deep knowing, a true belief that there is a higher purpose, a higher force. We are so small; we are just the messenger, just a channel.

On occasions it may be I have been having an off day myself, my mood has been off, I may have been under the weather and drained of energy, and felt a lack of empathy, and in truth my heart has not been in it. When this has happened the reading has been dry and fragmented. I feel like I am grasping at tangents. I am not a clear channel, the light does not pour through me, the light of truth and wisdom. At one stage in my career I would muddle through. My desire to help and please would spur me on.

However strong my will was, continuing to read without a clear focus can only cause dissatisfied customers and bad feedback.

After learning from experience and developing my own self-confidence, it was much easier to speak the truth and say, "I'm not having a good day, I feel unable to make a clear connection for you today, sorry. I didn't sleep well last night, my energy is low." Don't waste your time and energy, or the sitter's time and money. Honesty goes a lot further and is better appreciated.

The truth is, we must have plenty of energy ourselves to work with the energy of others. When making a connection with Spirit and our Spirit Guides it is our energy that they use to make a clear connection. If our energy is low, then that connection is not going to be clear and strong. I have come to realize that although my desire to help other people is strong, I must maintain my own health first.

I frequently come across a common error of thinking about the work involved with the Spirit Realm. We don't choose to work with Spirit; Spirit will choose to work with us! It is all about our intention. If Spirit cannot work with our energy then they won't. I often receive e-mails asking, why can I not see Spirit? Or hear Spirit? How do I develop further? I want to give messages from Spirit to loved ones? The problem is it is not enough to want. We must look at our full intentions, the love, the belief, the gratitude and the faith behind it all.

The best advice I can give, when it comes to developing psychic abilities, is to know you. This requires finding your centre, finding that peace. It is about love, yes love! Loving yourself is perhaps one of the hardest hurdles you may have to jump over within your lifetime, although very essential to your personal development, change and enlightenment.

For once you have learned to accept yourself for who you are, you recognize the perfections, you come to love the inner, then the outer beauty; it is such a powerful and overwhelming feeling to recognize that by design you are perfect, beautiful, whole, and loving. Once you have conquered this, you recognize this within others, and then your perceptions will be cleansed.

Learning to forgive wrongs in your life, and coming to understand that all experiences have been learning curves (even the bad ones); they are there to help us to grow, to teach us, to shape us in to who we are to become. We are all responsible for our own actions; it is our own free will how we choose to react from the effects of the past. It is cause and effect, Karma. Life is about learning; every possible situation is about learning, and growing.

Every experience and every challenge is a chance to expand and to grow. A true mystic will always find the positive in every situation, always looking at ways to expand the feeling of love, finding a peaceful centre and always a positive outcome. It is always the here and now that counts; it is the decisions in the present that affect the future. Development can be a beautiful journey of self-knowing. It is about learning to listen to your higher self, to trust and believe in your own abilities and in your own intuition.

The exercises, guides and meditations are all a way of helping to awaken the light within you. The door in our mind that we open as part of our spiritual protection ritual is just a metaphor for our mind's eye. In truth when I ask you to visual a door and open the door to your mind, I am asking you to open your mind's eye!

> **If the doors of perception were cleansed everything would appear to man as it is, infinite. For man has closed himself up, till he sees all things through narrow chinks of his cavern.**
> – Aldous Huxley (1894–1963), *The Doors of Perception*

While teaching Psychic Development, I practised the opening of the mind's eye. The results were that a large majority struggled to see and visualize their eye opening. This caused frustration as many students wanted to achieve the opening of the mind's eye.

Although when I ask the students to visualize the door to the mind opening up, this was easily attained. I had kept it to myself that this was just a metaphor for the mind's eye, and the acceptance of the door was easily digested.

After several weeks of maintaining the opening of the door in the mind, the students then returned to the visual exercise of opening the 'mind's eye'; the results were good. I explained that the door had been a metaphor for the 'mind's eye', and this was just symbolic of opening the Third Eye or Brow Chakra. The students could then clearly, and with ease, complete the exercise. I am not sure if it had been through fear, expectation and pressure which had caused bad results. But once the students found that their perceptions had been cleansed from the beginning, the light had been flooding in from the very start, they were able to visualize instantly.

Some writers and researchers, including HP Blavatsky, the founder of the Theosophical Society and the author of such fascinating works including, *The Secret Doctrine* and *Isis Unveiled*, have suggested that the third eye is in fact the partially dormant pineal gland, which resides between the two hemispheres of the brain. The pineal gland is said to secrete Dimethyltryptamine (DMT).

Science tells us that DMT is a naturally-occurring tryptamine and potent psychedelic drug, found not only in many plants, but also in trace amounts in the human body where its natural function is undetermined.

The focus is on the pineal gland, and the development of the Brow Chakra, its Sanskrit name being Agya Chakra. The belief is that when the stimulation of the Brow Chakra happens we awaken the pineal gland also, hence releasing DMT which brings a state of awareness including dreams, lucid dreaming, OBE (out of body experience), meditation, and visions.

Psychic Protection

When we start to develop our psychic abilities, we are opening ourselves up to all kinds of energies. We are sensitive to the energies and auras of others, and to the energy of Spirit.

The first lesson I teach is always about protection, safety and connection.

I always say the golden rule is, **'Like attracts like'**!

If we live life with good intentions and with care and empathy for others, if we are mindful and respectful, then the energy that we give out is the energy that we will find coming back to us.

This is a good rule and an important one for all to follow.

It is important to realize that we are powered by energy. Science tells us that organic matter can spoil and perish, but evidence also tells us that the energy that drives that matter still lives on, energy cannot be destroyed, energy only changes form.

We must keep in mind that there are many among us living a negative existence and we can pick up that energy.

It is not that negative energy of the living, or of spirit, can particularly place us in danger. It is that when you are unprotected to these energies, they can drain you, leaving you feeling:

- Drained/Lethargic/Irritable
- Depressed/Low in mood/Tearful/No hopes/ Even suicidal
- Hearing negative type voices
- Sickness/Dizziness
- Feeling under the weather
- Disturbed sleep and thoughts/Paranoia
- A feeling of being pulled out of bed while asleep.
- Forced down or unable to move, restricted.
- Physically being pushed.

I have been woken from my slumber to the sensation of being

pulled or yanked from my bed. It felt as if someone was literally pulling my arms up and really yanking me out of bed. This has also happened with my legs, from the bottom of the bed. I felt my head being pulled under the covers, and I couldn't breathe.

I have also awoken to the feeling of having what seemed like water splashed on my head. I woke up and I knew it was Spirit trying to grab my attention. I said, "Leave me alone, I'm sleeping." I went to the toilet and then continued with my sleep; feeling satisfied that the spirit who had woken me would now leave me alone. I was sound asleep and all of a sudden I was roused by a heavy sensation; I became aware of this feeling of being weighed down, I felt massively oppressed. I felt restricted in movement and in thought. I became slowly aware of the presence of a male spirit energy that was lying on top of me. It was non-sexual! It was very heavy, repressive, and seemed to take away my energy.

I shouted get off, get off, and it seemed I had to use all of my will to get up. I then prayed, using a mantra that I use when I have felt in need of protection, conjuring my Angel Guides and Spirit Guides:

Dear God, Jesus Christ and the Holy Spirit.
In love and light, in love and light, in love and light,
I call forward my Angel Guides and Spirit Guides to be
  with me now.
Protect me now.
Take away the bad that lingers here, take away the confused
  that is trapped here, and take away the negative energy
  that feeds here.
Dear God bless me with your love, light, and protection.
In love and light, in love and light, in love and light,
It is done, it is done, it is done.

The next day I performed a Spiritual House Cleansing, to cleanse my home of unwanted entities and negativities. In doing so I replenished my home with positivity, and the light and love of the cosmic universe. This brings a good energy and balance to the home, a good feeling. Everybody who comes to my home always tells me how good it feels, how nice my home is and how good the energy is. I tell them, "Oh, it's because I've cleaned up!" I recommend a good house cleansing once a month. I will cover this in the chapter **Spiritual House Cleansing**.

When starting any kind of spiritual based work we open ourselves up to the energies of other people and also to the energy of the spirit world.

I believe that the mind transcends the body; the mind and subconscious reality is a separate entity to the brain. When our physical reality has ended, I believe that our energy exists within the mind, a subconscious reality or The Collective Unconscious as theorized by Swiss psychiatrist Carl Gustav Jung.

The dream is a little hidden door in the innermost and most secret recesses of the soul, opening into that cosmic night which was psyche long before there was any ego-consciousness, and which will remain psyche no matter how far our ego-consciousness extends.
– Carl Jung

When connecting with Spirit in our Psychic work it is a mind to mind experience. With time and practice this recognition becomes stronger. Images, symbols and senses are sharper as we learn to become brighter channels.

It is important to sustain self-discipline when working on a psychic and spiritual level; we must learn how to tap into our consciousness, tuning in and tuning out. It simply would not be logical to walk around tuned in all day long; we would soon tire, and our energies would drain.

The following technique is a ritual that I follow, whenever I am opening to work. This is like an athlete warming up, a 100m sprinter would not start a race without first stretching; neither would I start any psychic or spiritual exercise without first opening and protecting myself.

Follow this outlined technique before any spiritual practice:

Grounding

Visualize roots coming out from your feet and pushing into the ground. See them going down deep, deep into the earth. The roots are like tree roots and these connect us with the earth and give us a solid feeling of being 'Grounded'.

Chakras

Focus your attention to the chakras and starting at the base open each one.

There are many ways of aligning ourselves and we will find what suits us with experience. Here it may help to see each chakra opening like a flower or a spinning disc. (See the chapter on **Chakras** for guidance.)

1   Red Flower – Base
2   Orange Flower – Sacral
3   Yellow Flower – Solar Plexus
4   Green Flower – Heart
5   Blue Flower – Throat
6   Indigo Flower – Brow
7   Violet Flower – Crown

Channel of Light

After the opening of the Crown Chakra, envision a channel of light reaching up to the heavens. It is a strand of light, like a ribbon. This reaches up and beyond. It is at this point. you declare:

I am a clear channel for light, wisdom and energy.

The Spiritual Door

This is your personal door; this is the door in your mind. Invent this as your own. My door has an open sign with locks and bolts. So when I am ready I can open it. I take off the lock and place the open sign on, then turn the key, open the door and let in the light. I am now open.

Visualize your door; this may change over time; when you are ready, open up.

The purpose of the door serves to access other levels of consciousness, especially through meditation.

I say here:

I am open and ready to receive (repeat 3 times).

I work for the highest good, in truth and light to bring help, guidance, wisdom and love from above. I ask for protection and guidance always. Thank you, Amen.

Protection

I now see a shell, like an egg of light; this is an Auric Egg. It's light may be pearly, it may be pink, or have many colours like a rainbow. The colour suits you. You will feel protected, warm and comforted. This shell of light surrounds you and encompasses you. This is your shell of protection. Thank your Guides and your Angels for their protection. Even if you are unaware of them at this time, believe that they are there with you.

You are now open, protected, and ready to practise psychic development.

Important Closing Down
Always Close Your Door!

Close up your door, lock it, bolt it, put on the closed sign, etc...

Bring your Roots back up from the earth.

Visualize yourself stepping into a sleeping bag and zipping it up. OR

Imagine yourself sat inside a flower (any flower), and the petals closing up around you. OR

A cloak of protection wrapped around you, with a hood pulled over.

Grounding yourself... it helps after spiritual based work to stamp your feet, clap your hands, drink some water, and maybe eat a biscuit or get some fresh air.

Personally: I visualize myself sat inside a golden yellow tulip. Inside, I curl up within the cup of this beautiful flower. The golden glow that the tulip produces induces a feeling of warmth and comfort. I see the tulip gently swaying to and fro in a light breeze. Once curled up I visualize the petals closing up all around me creating a barrier of protection. There I am inside of my golden yellow tulip protected.

There are all kinds of ways to protect yourself; it comes with experience.

Whenever you feel you need protecting from negative forces, whenever you feel yourself becoming drained, place yourself inside the shell of light and say a quick prayer of guidance:

Angels, Angels, Angels, please protect me from harm.

Chakras

Chakras are energy centres running in alignment with the spinal column.

We each have seven chakras; each functions like a vast halo channelling energy between our spiritual and physical bodies.

Indian Seers named these 'Chakram', meaning 'wheel', as they appear to be spinning wheels of light.

By connecting our physical body with the Energy Bodies/Aura, the chakra processes emotion and thoughts as a form of energy.

Loving thoughts enable the energy to flow freely creating a feeling of well-being and health, whereas fearful and negative thoughts cause blocks in the chakras and in the energy flow.

We open our chakra energy centres when working psychically; we open ourselves to the energies of others and also to the energies of spirit on the Spiritual/Astral Plane that can be felt through our Energy Body/Aura which passes through our chakra centres.

Each chakra has a different function, serving to process different feelings and different types of energy.

When working with our chakras for psychic work we open our chakras with 'intention', starting at the bottom with the Base/Red Chakra.

The chakras can be seen as spinning discs or wheels, although it helps with psychic development to visualize our chakras as flowers opening and beginning to bloom.

It is essential to take your time over this subject. Remember, Rome wasn't built in a day. It takes time and practice to accomplish goals. Don't give up! With practice the opening of chakras will become instant.

Take your time and visualize each one, starting at the base, at the bottom of your spine imagine a Red Rose beginning to bloom and so on and so on.

Below are the Seven Chakras and their associated colours and explanation.

- **Root Chakra – Red**

Located at the base of the spine, this chakra forms our foundation. It represents the element earth, and is therefore related to our survival instincts, and to our sense of grounding and connection to our bodies and the physical plane. Ideally this chakra brings us health, prosperity, security, and dynamic presence.

- **Sacral Chakra – Orange**

The second chakra, located in the abdomen, lower back, and sexual organs, is related to the element water, and to emotions and sexuality. It connects us to others through feeling, desire, sensation, and movement. Ideally this chakra brings us fluidity and grace, depth of feeling, sexual fulfilment, and the ability to accept change.

- **Solar Plexus Chakra – Yellow**

This chakra is known as the power chakra, located in the solar plexus. It rules our personal power, will, and autonomy, as well as our metabolism. When healthy, this chakra brings us energy, effectiveness, spontaneity, and non-dominating power.

- **Heart Chakra – Green**

This chakra is called the Heart Chakra and is the middle chakra in a system of seven. It is related to love and is the integrator of opposites in the psyche: mind and body, male and female, persona and shadow, ego and unity. A healthy fourth chakra allows us to love deeply, feel compassion and empathy, and also have a deep sense of peace and centeredness.

- **Throat Chakra – Blue**

This is the chakra located in the throat and is thus related to communication and creativity. Here we experience the world symbolically through vibration, such as the vibration of sound representing language.

- **Brow Chakra – Indigo**

This chakra is known as the Brow Chakra or Third Eye centre. It is related to the act of seeing, both physically and intuitively. As such it opens our psychic faculties and our understanding of archetypal levels. When healthy it allows us to see clearly; in effect, letting us 'see the bigger picture'.

- **Crown Chakra – Violet**

This is the Crown Chakra that relates to consciousness as pure awareness. Some refer to it as a 'God Source'. It is our connection to the greater world beyond, to a timeless, space-less place of all-knowing. When developed, this chakra brings us knowledge, wisdom, understanding, spiritual connection, and bliss.

The exploration of the Chakras, Auras and the Energy Bodies is a vast subject to be explored and I do recommend learning about this interesting subject in further detail.

Chakra Cleansing

Cleansing the chakras is necessary because of the different energies floating around you, all of that unhappiness you worked up in an argument or the pessimistic influences that are around you. All of these things stay around you like metal attracted to a magnet. Because you are 'sensitive', and because you are opening up your 'chakra' energy centres, you will come in to contact with some 'dirty' energies.

You are now beginning to work with your own, and other energies, on a regular basis. Using your chakras is an important part of your work; it is important to look after them and keep them clean and in balance so they are able to process energy flow efficiently.

Think of that favourite cup. You wouldn't keep drinking your tea out of it without ever washing it up. The tea stains, grime and residue would soon build up until you are forced to clean this cup until sparkling again.

When regular cleansing of the chakras occurs, you will begin to notice that your energy flows better and you become much more intuitive. Your senses and feelings are much more in tune. You will begin to feel better in balance. The first time I cleansed my chakras it was while in meditation, it was totally unplanned for. Once again I was on my path to enlightenment, travelling with my Guides, learning new and useful tools as I went.

I found myself at a healing pool, with crystal clear waters. I submerged myself within this pool and I could feel the cool and cleansing sensation all around me. I sank deep within this pool and I realized that the water was there to heal me, to fix and correct my perceptions.

I came back to the shore and sat for a while; it was at this place that I met with my Guardian Angel.

My Guardian Angel drew my attention back to the chalice

that she held above my head. Inside the chalice was liquid light and liquid love. This is how I can explain it. My Guardian Angel poured the light over me from the chalice; this divine fluid was the brightest, whitest light I had ever seen.

The light consumed me; starting from my crown, it seemed to fill me, and with every breath that I took, the light filled my body, my mind and my soul. The feeling was wonderful, the many emotions that I felt rushing my energy system, love, joy and happiness. I felt overcome with beauty. The light seemed to embrace me. I felt drawn to look at my chakras and the colours here. I could see that they were now spinning with ease and the more I focused the more I could see the light bringing them to full vibrancy. My Angel placed the chalice in an upright position once again and the divine light returned up and out of my crown, leaving me feeling refreshed and vibrant.

I have never forgotten the sensations which I felt the first time that I cleansed my chakras; it was truly an unforgettable experience. Over time and with experience, I have learned and come across other methods to achieve the same result.

It is essential to try and cleanse the chakras often; at least once a month is recommended. I do feel better when I have cleansed my chakras and always feel that I give better readings when I take my time to do this. My connection seems to be sharper as the energy flow is more fluid.

Guided Meditation – Chakra Cleansing

- It is advisable to wear loose fitting clothes for comfort, and please make sure that you have visited the toilet beforehand. The aim is to rid yourself of as many distractions as possible.
- Focus on your grounding and psychic protection exercise beforehand.
- Start the meditation by playing some gentle and relaxing music. Now lay or sit comfortably, hands at your side or in your lap.
- Once you have accomplished a comfortable sitting position, take three cleansing, deep breaths.
- With each breath, allow yourself to deeply relax.
- There is nothing you must do now. You are allowing yourself 15–20 minutes relaxation, this is OK. There is nothing to tend to; let go of the day, this is your time.
- Relax deeply... breathe in and out at a comfortable and relaxed pace. Allow your breathing to relax you further.
- Relax your arms, relax your legs and relax your shoulders.
- If you find yourself losing focus then return your attention back to your breathing and relax your shoulders.
- Take some time to focus on the door in your mind. When you're ready walk through this, stepping out on to a path, walk down the path to a gate, open the gate, and walk through it.
- Find yourself in a golden meadow of tranquil peace and serenity. Find somewhere warm, comfortable and peaceful to sit.
- Visualize a ball of pure, bright and golden light that hovers nearby. As you watch this light it comes closer to you, and as you focus on this light you draw it close. You find you become fascinated and mesmerized by the

brilliance of this beautiful light.

- You can feel love, happiness, joy, truth and wisdom that are contained within this light. The light is drawn above you, above your Crown Chakra, and radiates its beautiful intenseness all around you.
- You breathe this light in... Breathe the light into your lungs, like glittering air. This light is magnificent, the Light of the Divine, of the Universe and Cosmic Energy, this is the Light of God.
- Breathe this light into you, allowing it to dispel any negativity. Allow this light to fill you with positivity, love, light, joy, wisdom and truth... As you breathe in this light you can feel your energies being cleansed, your energies being renewed and your spirit being lifted.
- Take a few moments to bathe in this light and visualize this divine light washing over your chakras and surrounding your aura. Visualize your chakras gleaming in their natural colours.
- When the light has replenished you, and your chakras are cleansed, the light will withdraw back up through your body and through the Crown Chakra, returning to a ball of light above your head. Release this and watch it hover back over the meadow.
- When you feel you have finished with your meditation, return to your gate, walk back up your path and back through your door.
- Always close your door on return. Practise the closing down and psychic protection exercise as provided.
- After meditation it is recommended to take a drink, clap your hands, and place yourself firmly back on to the earth plane once again.

Remember to write down your journey in your spiritual diary.

Spirit Guides

We have all heard of the term Spirit Guide and we have all heard of Guardian Angels, but what are they? What is their purpose? How do we know them or contact them?

In this chapter, I explore Spirit Guides and Guardian Angels to help bring a little light of understanding into this area. I feel it is a necessary part of psychic exploration and development to discover and work with Spirit Guides.

The Encarta Concise Dictionary describes a spirit to be a supernatural entity, a paranormal supernatural being that does not have a physical body.

Spirit Guides are evolved beings who have lived a physical existence. A Spirit Guide's purpose is to help, guide, teach and protect us. Our Spirit Guides can take many guises from children to animals.

Angel Guides differ to Spirit Guides. Angel Guides or Guardian Angels are beings of light. They have never lived an earth life, a physical existence. Guardian Angels are described as thoughts of God, an existence of his conscience love. An Angel's purpose is to guide and to protect us.

The word 'Angel' in English is a fusion of the Old English word 'engel' and the Old French 'angele'. The word Angel itself has originated from the Latin word 'angelus', which both of these words have derived from. In Hebrew Angel is 'mal'ak' and in Greek 'aggelos'. All of these terms are translated in to the meaning 'Messenger'. Many of the major religions all over the world make reference to Angels and Messengers from God. These religions include Islam, Judaism, Christianity and Spiritualism. Angels are Messengers from God.

In Islam, Angels are described as: "light-based creatures, created from light by God to serve and worship Him."

These many religions share many views on Angels and their

purpose, and there is always a consistent theory that Angels are Messengers from God and that it is clear that there is a set order or hierarchy that exists between Angels, defined by the assigned purpose and various tasks to which Angels are commanded by God. There are many, many Angels, and their purposes are said to differ. Healing Angels, Protection Angels, Angels of Love and Angels of the Arts; Angels have many purposes.

We know of many Angels all with various names and purposes for example:

Michael: Meaning 'Who is like God'. Archangel Michael protects us.

Gabriel: Meaning 'Strength of God'. Archangel Gabriel brings us wisdom, strength and hope.

Raphael: Meaning 'God Heals'. Archangel Raphael brings the light of healing to us.

It is thought that we have to invite Angels to help us because to intervene in our lives without invitation would be to interfere in our free will.

And the angel answering said unto him, I am Gabriel, that stand in the presence of God; and am sent to speak unto thee, and to shew thee these glad tidings.
– Luke 1:19

According to Theosophical doctrine, Spirit Guides are persons who have lived many former lifetimes, paid their Karmic debts, and advanced beyond a need to reincarnate. Many devotees believe that Spirit Guides are chosen on 'the other side' by human beings who are about to incarnate and wish assistance.

The Jungian and Gestalt schools of psychology used guided imagery to access inner wisdom. In a technique called "Dialogue with the Sage or Inner Teacher", patients were placed in relaxed surroundings and were encouraged to imagine themselves in a comfortable and pleasant environment where they would then meet a person of great wisdom. The patient is then encouraged to allow a dialogue to emerge spontaneously. Information is emitted through the mind through feelings, images or sounds producing valuable information. Authors, artists and business people alike employ these methods for inspiration.

Inner Teachers or Guides can arise rather spontaneously and have a life changing impact. Some major historical figures have been documented to have been directed by such Guides, Gandhi, Socrates, Carl Jung and William Blake. Helena Blavatsky talked about being guided by the Mahatma of India and Alice Bailey called her Spirit Guide the Tibetan. They all reported that they were advised by Inner Guides or Teachers who arose from the depths of their own psyche.

An understanding heart is everything in a teacher, and cannot be esteemed highly enough. One looks back with appreciation to the brilliant teachers, but with gratitude to those who touched our human feeling.
– Carl Jung (1875 – 1961)

Through meditation I have taken many journeys with my Spirit Guides and spoke with them. I have learned many lessons from them.

When meeting Spirit Guides and Guardian Angels the experience should always be emotionally rewarding; the experience is always fulfilling. You will never feel that it is negative; the information that is gathered in the presence of your Guides will always be inspiring and enlightening.

You will have many Guides in this lifetime, often one of your Guides may become the dominating presence, the 'Gatekeeper'. Remember there are no limitations.

In fact while working with my Guides, I have learned that I

have eleven Guides. This number is of great significance and importance. Numerology plays a huge role within esoteric mysticism, and especially the Pythagoras theories. The universe is mathematically coordinated, there are no coincidences, and everything is timed to perfection.

I am told I have 11 Guides and in numerology we add: $1 + 1 = 2$; the number 2 brings balance, structure and duality. Number 2 is the symbol of partnerships and combining opposites. When I am brought into the equation, when I am sat together with my Guides, together we equal 12 – this brings: $1 + 2 = 3$. The number three in numerology is the communicator, three is the trinity, the mind, the body and the spirit. I am the connection, the medium. I am the link with the physical world and reality. I am seated on the edge of the veil.

I am also told that our number together 'twelve' has a great significance with astrology and the zodiac. That together we fit like constellations, we bring all the elements of the zodiac together. It is our many unique elements that fit and complement the spiritual partnership that exists between us.

Some mediums can be quite guarded or secretive about sharing knowledge of their Spirit Guides. However, I feel it is good to speak openly about such subjects; the more we are aware of our invisible helpers the more acceptable it becomes.

It has taken me many years to establish a firm connection with my Guides and many years of practising the art of meditation. I have found that this practice and perseverance has been very rewarding.

Many people who visit me will enquire about Spirit Guides. They often ask if I can tell them who their Spirit Guide is or if they have someone watching over them. The answer is yes, we all have a Guardian Angel on our shoulder and we all have Spirit Guides. However, I don't ever tell people who their Guides are. I often give words of comfort and guidance with some small inclinations.

Have you ever seen twinkling lights from the corner of your eyes or above another person?

While teaching psychic and spiritual development class I encourage contact with Spirit Guides. I never tell my students who their Spirit Guides are. I may confirm questions that are asked. I feel that it is important to find all about your Spirit Guides for yourself, because the experience is very personal and also very rewarding.

In my personal learning and development I have joined many groups, and sat in many mediumship circles. I always wanted to learn and understand as much as I could. I would take what I needed and disregard the rest. I would move on when I realized there was nothing more to learn from that particular place. In one group, I was told my Spirit Guide was a nun, a nun, in an old-fashioned habit, maybe Roman Catholic? I have never seen a nun with me, and like I have explained, I have worked with my Guides intensely. I'm not sure if it is the fact that I doubted it from the beginning or if it was ever really true in the first place. It is this reason that I feel it is important to encourage contact and knowledge of Spirit Guides rather than be given information.

I receive e-mails everyday with all kinds of comments, questions and queries. I received one e-mail where I was asked if I could confirm the identity of a Spirit Guide. The gentleman who had sent me the e-mail claimed that he had felt that his Spirit Guide was Amelia Earhart.

While helping my husband discover more about his Spirit Guides, my husband's Guide appeared to him like a cartoon image in his mind's eye. This doesn't mean that it is an illustration of the mind or an illusion. Our Guides present themselves in ways that we feel comfortable with or that we can relate to.

Our Guides, whether they are Native Americans, citizens from the fallen Atlantis, Roman Catholic nuns or Ancient Egyptians, will communicate with us and present images to us that we understand in our language and in our lifetime. We must understand at this point, our Guides have been sent to help, guide, teach and protect us. They are evolved supreme beings who stand in the light of truth and love.

It may take a while to really develop your links with your Spirit Guides. The more you work, meditate and link with your Guides the more you will come to know them. To begin with, your Spirit Guides may not identify themselves by name; this may happen in time. Your Guide may, for example, identify themselves by a certain smell they give you when they are around, or a certain feeling, certain images and symbols.

Always keep notes in your spiritual diary of any experiences, especially after meditating with Spirit Guides.

- What did you feel?
- What did you experience?
- Did you sense anything?
- Did you see or smell anything?
- Did you hear any sounds?

I recommend entering into a meditative state with the intention of meeting your Spirit Guide. It is the intention that brings success. I also recommend meditating with music. Spirit meditation CDs are available to purchase and are often enhanced with tribal sounds, drums, flutes and pan pipes; this music seems help the meditation experience and promotes a deeper and relaxed state, helping with connection and clarity in vision.

Guided Meditation – Spirit Guide

- Start this meditation first by grounding and using the spiritual protection exercise provided.
- I recommend wearing loose fitting clothing for the benefit of relaxation.
- Visit the bathroom before entering meditation; the aim is to take away as many distractions as possible.
- It is recommended that a glass of water is placed at your side for after the meditation is finished.
- Always start the mediation by sitting or lying in a relaxed position. Take three cleansing breaths and allow yourself to deeply relax.
- I recommend using meditation music, spirit meditation or tribal sounds.
- Breathe deeply until you are relaxed then regulate breathing... if you wander off with 'mind chatter' just keep coming back to your breathing and relax (I always become aware that I have tensed my legs and shoulders); just relax and breathe.
- Relax deeply... breathe in and out at a comfortable and relaxed pace. Allow your breathing to relax you further. As you breathe and relax into the meditation your intention must be to meet your Spirit Guide. It is this intention that will draw your Spirit Guide close to you.
- Relax your arms, relax your legs, relax your shoulders, relax your hands and relax your feet down to your toes. Deeply relax allowing yourself to let go into a comfortable state of calm and contentment.
- When ready and deeply relaxed, walk through the door in your mind. Visualize the path that you step out on to, walk to the end of the path and walk through the gate.
- You find yourself stood between two paths.

- One path stretches to the left, this is to the west and the other path stretches to the right, this is to the east.
- To the west you can see the path leads to a river. A boat rests peacefully at the water's edge and there is a bridge that leads to the other side. There is a sense of serenity and mystery here.
- To the east you can see that the path leads to the wilderness, a forest of azure that seems to be thick with expectation and life and knowledge.
- You will feel a pull within you; take any direction now.
- Who do you meet? What do you see here? Is there anyone on the bridge? What is on the other side? Do you see anybody on the river? Do you travel downstream in the boat? Where does this take you?
- What do you learn in the forest? Who do you meet? Do you smell anything? Do you hear anything? What do you see here? Who do you meet here?
- Take your time and let your mind roam free.
- Don't question your experience, just allow the experience to happen. Relax and breathe.
- When you feel you are complete in your journey make your way back though the gate and back through your door.
- Always close your door on return. Practise the closing down and psychic protection exercise as provided.
- After meditation it is recommended to take a drink, clap your hands, and place yourself firmly back on to the earth plane once again.

Remember to write down your journey in your spiritual diary.
The more you practise this meditation with the intention of connecting with your Spirit Guide, the more successful you will be. Don't give up if you do not find instant results. It can take weeks and months to gain a strong bond with your Spirit Guides, but once you have found it, it will be with you for life.

Guided Meditation – Guardian Angel

- Start this meditation first by grounding and using the spiritual protection exercise provided.
- I recommend wearing loose fitting clothing for the benefit of relaxation.
- Visit the bathroom before entering meditation; the aim is to take away as many distractions as possible.
- It is recommended that a glass of water is placed at your side for after the meditation is finished.
- Always start the mediation by sitting relaxed. Take three cleansing breaths and allow yourself to deeply relax.
- I recommend using relaxing soothing music.
- Breathe deep until you are relaxed then regulate your breathing... If you wander off with 'mind chatter' just keep coming back to your breathing and relaxing (I always become aware that I have tensed my legs and shoulders); just relax and breathe.
- Relax deeply... Breathe in and out at a comfortable and relaxed pace. Allow your breathing to relax you further. As you breathe and relax into the meditation your intention must be to meet with your Guardian Angel. It is this intention that will draw your Guardian Angel close to you.
- Relax your arms, relax your legs, relax your shoulders, relax your hands and relax your feet down to your toes. Deeply relax, allowing yourself to let go into a comfortable state of calm and contentment.
- When ready and deeply relaxed walk through the door in your mind. Visualize the path that you step out on to, walk to the end of the path and walk through the gate.
- You are now surrounded by mist. This mist is very thick.
- In the distance you see a beacon of light. This is your

guiding light and with all your faith you follow this light.

- As you walk through the mist you can see the light becoming brighter and closer. Your feelings tell you that you're on the right path as your trust and faith deepen in the guiding light.

- You can see nothing else but the guiding light; the mist obscures the path, but your faith still remains. You have such a wonderful feeling about the light and you know that your intuition is serving you well. You are allowing yourself to follow your feelings, to follow your heart.

- The light becomes brighter and brighter and your feelings become more intense; you are overwhelmed by a sense of love, truth, wisdom and positivity.

- The mist clears and you find you are stood in front of a beautiful white ethereal temple.

- You enter this temple, allowing yourself to take in the feelings, images and energy that are contained here.

- Within the centre of the temple there is a room that is filled with light. You enter the room and notice that the feeling is light and angelic. There is a seat positioned at the window. You take a seat here. You feel warm and comfortable as you feel you are sinking down into your seat.

- You are relaxed, and this room emanates light, a healing light, and as you relax here you feel all tension leave you.

- You focus your attention on the angelic light and presence that begins to fill the room. Your guiding light. You feel a sense of love, the beauty of wisdom and truth. Your Guardian Angel appears to you now.

- Allow the appearance, or any thoughts, feelings or any other information to come to you instantly.

- Take your time here. This is your journey, this is your experience. Absorb all feelings and emotions.

- When you feel that you have finished, find yourself back at your gate, walk through it, back up the path and back through your door. Remember to close your door!

We may find it takes many visits to the temple to find out more information about your Guardian Angel. Allow any instant information to wash over you. You may become aware of your Guardian Angel's name instantly or in time. The same applies for the gender of your Angel. You may want to ask your Guardian Angel a question, or you may accept the guidance that your Guardian Angel offers you. Our Guardian Angels will always speak with love, truth and wisdom. The first initial visit may be for healing purposes. In time and with practice you can allow yourself to speak with and to journey anywhere with your Guardian Angel.

Write your experience down in your spiritual diary.

Symbols and Clairvoyance

Clairvoyance is from the French word meaning clear vision or clear visibility. Clairvoyant impressions come in visions or images through the mind's eye, often called the second sight.

This can be described and likened to a postcard or photo shop, where we are able to catch quick glimpses of a photograph or postcard within the mind's eye, a glimpse, a fleeting impression, or a vivid vision.

We must learn to use our intuition when working with the images that come to us. We must also learn to understand the images that we are receiving and learn to interpret them. Through experience we become brighter channels, and the symbols, images and visions do become clearer.

We all have our own unique lives and life experiences, meaning that something may be more relevant to you than it would be to me. This is your path and your learning curve and a very fulfilling and exciting one at that; this is personal to you, all I can do is be but a guide.

Clairvoyance is clear seeing, but we experience many senses when developing this amazing gift and ability; here I have explored this in a little more depth.

What is Clairvoyance?

Clairvoyance

Taken from 17th century French (Clair) meaning 'clear' and (Voyance) meaning 'visibility', it is the apparent ability to gain information about an object, location, person or physical event through means other than the known human senses, a form of extra-sensory perception (ESP). A person said to have the ability of clairvoyance is referred to as a clairvoyant. One Who Sees!

Extra Sensory Perception is a term used to describe any mental faculty that allows a person to acquire knowledge about the world without the use of the known senses. The term ESP is said to have originally derived from an early pioneer of parapsychology, Joseph Rhine from Harvard University.

It was also the same Joseph Rhine and his colleague Karl Zener that designed the now known Zener Cards. This set of 25 symbolic cards were used to measure ESP and also Telepathy.

The words 'clairvoyance' and 'psychic' are often used to refer to many different kinds of paranormal sensory experiences, but there are more specific names.

Clairvoyance is to see, or far seeing, future seeing, often termed as a second sight, as the images, visions or impressions that occur are within the mind's eye, or the third eye (Brow Chakra). Clairvoyance is often associated with seeing events of the future.

Clairsentience (feeling/touching)

Clairsentience is a form of ESP wherein a person acquires psychic knowledge primarily by means of feeling. The word is from the French (Clair) meaning 'clear'; (sentience) 'feeling', and is ultimately derived from the Latin Clarus, 'clear', sentiens, derived from sentire, 'to feel'.

Generally the term refers to a person who can feel the vibration and energies of other people. There are many different degrees of clairsentience ranging from the perception of diseases of other people to the thoughts or emotions of other people. The ability differs from the third eye in that this kind of ability cannot have a vivid picture in the mind. Instead, a very vivid feeling can form.

Psychometry is related to clairsentience. The word stems from psyche and metric, which means 'to measure with the mind'.

Clairaudience (hearing/listening)

Clairaudience is taken from the late 17th century French (Clair), clear and (audience). Where a person acquires information by paranormal auditory means. It is considered to be a part and form of clairvoyance. Clairaudience is essentially the ability to hear in a paranormal manner, as opposed to paranormal seeing (clairvoyance) and feeling (clairsentience). Clairaudient people have psi-mediated hearing. Clairaudience does not refer to actual perception of sound, but instead indicates impressions of the 'inner mental ear' similar to the way many people think words without having auditory impressions. But it may also refer to actual perception of sounds such as voices, tones, music and noises which are not apparent to other humans or to recording equipment. For instance, a clairaudient person might claim to hear the voices or thoughts of the spirits of persons who are deceased.

Clairalience (smelling)
Clairalience is a form of ESP wherein a person acquires psychic knowledge primarily by means of smelling.

Claircognizance (knowing)
Claircognizance is when a person acquires psychic knowledge primarily by means of intrinsic knowledge. It is the ability to know something without knowing how or why you know it. This is that psychic ability, that intuition, that hunch, that knowing.

Clairgustance (tasting)
Clairgustance is defined as an ability that allegedly allows someone to taste a substance without putting anything in one's mouth. It is claimed that those who possess this ability are able to perceive the essence of a substance from the spiritual or ethereal realms through taste.

While working with my clairvoyance I am working with my intuition and instincts; this is my basic trust and belief. I am also working with images, visions, impressions and symbols that are brought into my mind's eye.

I am working with the feelings and senses that I feel through my Heart Chakra. What do I feel? What do I sense?

I am listening to thoughts, words, sounds that are brought to me via the Throat Chakra, at my point of communication.

I also trust my gut feeling, my hunch, what I feel I just 'know' deep within, what I trust in and believe. This is processed through my Solar Plexus Chakra.

I may smell tobacco, perfume or other fragrances. These smells can be subtle hints to let us know that we have connected with Spirit. Spirit provides us with clues to give as evidence of their existence in the afterlife.

While I am working clairvoyantly, my chakra system, my spiritual body is also working too, processing energy, senses, feelings, images and symbols.

We must remember we are a channel.

Symbols

Below I have given a few definitions of my own symbols for example. However, it is important for you to start a diary of your own symbols and their meaning. Please keep in mind that symbols often draw our attention to matters in the sitter's life. We often draw upon our own personal experiences too.

For example: if we see our own mothers or grandmothers our attention is drawn to our sitter's mother or grandmother.

I once was reading for a lady and I saw Brian Clough in my mind's eye. I thought, why am I seeing this. I connect Brian to Nottingham Forest FC as he used to be the manager. So I asked my sitter, "Do you have links to Nottingham?" Yes, her family lived there, and she was to visit in the next week.

Sometimes we relate to personal references to link with our sitters. I had a lady with me one evening and I kept hearing what sounded like Holly. I thought, what is this? Is this a reference to Christmas or a name? So I said, "I have the name Holly," but as soon as I had spoken, a vision of my mum's dog 'Ollie' appeared in my mind's eye. Ollie had been a little Yorkshire terrier. I then revealed I was seeing this type of dog and the lady had two, and had kept this breed of dog most of her life.

Learning to trust and have confidence in your own intuition is what it's all about; that is how we develop our psychic ability. When I first started out, I remember during one of my first readings I had a repetitive thought in my mind; I wanted to say to the gentleman, "Do you still live in the pub?" But my belief was not strong, and I thought I may offend him in case it was some reference to a drinking problem. You know, as it turned out, he did used to live in and manage a pub.

Recently, I was giving a reading for a lady and as I looked at her I had a vision of reindeers. My Guide kept repeating the word Lapland. It was just two weeks before Christmas and I thought my mind could be swamped with Christmas, but my strong belief has always shown me to trust my intuitive thoughts. I knew my Guides were working with me and helping to bring these clair-voyant images, and my clairaudience was working well because I could hear the words Lapland. I was then shown Bambi. The image of Bambi reinforced the reindeer, but also added a childlike influence. My instincts were telling me it was a child visiting Lapland where the reindeer live.

I told my client what I was seeing and I was right, she had just been to Lapland with her sick daughter. From here I was able to channel hope, and guidance about her sick child.

We are often given signals that direct us to where we need be in our sitter's life; for instance these signals gave me direction to my sitter's daughter. This is why my sitter had come to me; because she wanted guidance in this area, she wanted words that would help heal, inspire and give her a positive outlook. The fact that my Guides had shown me Lapland just helped my sitter to realize I was making a connection with her.

Often I may receive signals in the way of names. Sometimes these names may point to the people my sitter works with; then I know the direction I am given is to look at my sitter's work, career and goals.

Below are some common symbols and their meanings. Remember you must always use your own intuition to interpret your own symbols.

- **Airplane** – Suggests long distant travel, holiday.
- **Baby** – Often predicts the birth of a child.
- **Children** – To see lots of children often suggests work in childcare or teaching.
- **Stop sign** – The need to slow down, sometimes caution to think ahead before action.
- **Green light** – All go, good outcome.
- **Hearts** – Love, affection, romance, relationships.
- **Dove** – Peace and a peaceful solution to be met.
- **Motorway/Roads** – Travel, journey or distant issues.
- **Bridge** – Repairing emotional damage, good outcomes, and peaceful resolutions.
- **Broken Bridges** – The need to make amends, communication and compromise.
- **Piggy Bank/Coins** – Money, need to budget, money for that rainy day.
- **Books** – Study, course, learning, education and exams.
- **Sunrise** – New beginnings, fresh starts, a fresh outlook.
- **Sunset** – Endings, partings.
- **Dark clouds** – Depression, sadness, loneliness, anger, the need to forgive.
- **Rain and storm** – Tears and troubles, anger and arguments.
- **Bird in a cage** – Oppression, feeling trapped, a dominating force.
- **Bird in flight** – The need for freedom. Travel plans.
- **Gold rings** – Marriage and commitment.
- **The Moon** – Dreams, emotional issues, mental conflicts and lethargy.

Spiritual House Cleansing

Smudging

The ritual of smudging can be defined as 'Spiritual House Cleansing'. Smudging is the common name given to the Sacred Smoke Bowl Blessing, a powerful cleansing technique from the Native American tradition. However, the burning of herbs for emotional, psychic, and spiritual purification is common practice in many religious, healing, and spiritual traditions.

The smoke attaches itself to negative energy. As the smoke clears, it takes the negative energy with it, releasing it to regenerate into something more positive. Tests have also shown that the smoke of burning sage literally changes the ionization polarity of the air.

Sage has historically been used in smudging rituals as a means of invoking purification, protection, longevity, and immortality. The burning of sage is a popular practice espoused by various healing and spiritual groups. The word sage – salvia – comes from the Latin word 'salvare', which translated means 'To heal'. The healing properties in sage come from antibiotic agents. Some people boil sage and drink the water as a tea. Relief can be found in the smoke for sinus congestion and pain and even for migraine headaches.

Sage can be bought as smudging sticks in bundles from as little as £2 from any good New Age store. An alternative to sage is mugwort or cedar and juniper.

I perform a spiritual cleansing of my home when I can feel myself becoming drained of energy. I usually can feel my home becoming a little heavy or sometimes I can sense something that is lingering.

When there are energies in and out with problems, woes, mental congestion, over time that residue will linger and that is just from those in the physical world.

After I have performed the Spiritual House Cleansing the home feels lighter and welcoming, the atmosphere is replenished. If I leave my home to become 'dirty' I leave myself prone to psychic attack.

To perform your Spiritual House Cleansing you will need a Sage Smudging Stick. These are bought in a tied-up prepared bundle and can sometimes be bought as a mixture, i.e. sage and cedar, sage and lavender. I recommend garden sage or white sage; these are the most two common varieties but if you are unsure ask your supplier and I'm sure they will be pleased to advise you.

I usually start at the top of my home and work down.

I light the sage and blow to produce smoke; I suggest that you carry a bowl for the sage to sit in. Often it helps to fan the smoke around, and traditionally this would be done with a large feather. If you have one this is excellent, if not, don't worry an envelope is ideal!

Choose a room to start in. You must start your Spiritual House Cleansing with good intentions and love in your heart.

I now pray and invoke the healing light of God.

With the love and light of God (repeat 3 times)
Bless me with your light and protection.
Bless my home and bless this space.
In the light of love and of truth I call forward my Angels and my Spirit Guides. I pray for blessings of love and protection, bless my home and dispel all negativity that lingers here.
Take away any harmful force, remove any negative energy, it is with you.
I thank you for your presence, for your love, your guidance, your light and your protection.
In love and light (repeat 3 times)
With heaven's help

It is Done (repeat 3 times).

I also like to say the Lord's Prayer, but this is just my preference, because of my background. Feel free to say your own prayer.

Taking your sage smudging stick, go from room to room repeating the same invocation.

I usually end in the kitchen, which is situated on the ground floor at the back of my house, where I open the back door and as a ritual I wave goodbye to all the energies that were inside my home. It's as if I am confirming to myself that "it is done"! My home is clean of all that energy. All that residue energy has now been chased out. As I let the smoke out all that energy is trapped within the sage smoke and that smoke is now floating out of my back door into the fresh air; it is a release.

As the smoke clears, the sage acts as a purifier and healer; your home should now feel cleansed. Feel the light and subtle energy shift.

Methods for Psychic Development

In this chapter we look at developing the psychic abilities using practical methods like reading for other people.

In teaching Psychic Development Courses, I used the 5 Points of Power and Wisdom as a background because without this essential philosophy I believe personal growth, progress and enlightenment would be lost.

I also used practical exercises as tools of focus to help stretch the intuitive mind. Such exercises bring good, interesting and rewarding results.

It is important to mark progress by taking notes in your spiritual diary! This way you are able to see your own progress and build self-esteem and confidence.

While teaching, the energy within my classes was always filled with fun and laughter. It is good to keep this in mind; have fun with your practice, no pressure, especially when you are learning with others. It is not a race or a competition. In fact we will never get to the finish line; life is a continuous opportunity for learning and growing.

We may all be gifted, but how we choose to work with those gifts may differ from person to person. What is right for one person may not feel necessarily right for another.

Here I have outlined practical exercises that can be used alone, as part of group work or in pairs.

Flower Reading

With flower reading it is important to pick the flower yourself. Be especially drawn to that flower. Keep the flower with you; it is recommended that you wrap the flower in paper when attending a group so others cannot identify your flower. It is recommended that the flowers remain separate, so that the energy of your flower is kept intact.

Appoint a group leader who will keep the flowers separate and anonymous and who will then bring the flowers into the practice room at the start of the readings.

When giving a flower reading, please keep in mind the guidelines below, but remain in touch with your intuition. As with any other kind of reading, this is a focus for your mind, a key to unlocking your potential, and a channel for your psychic awareness.

Let go, just allow yourself to flow, follow your feelings, your gut, and your intuitions. If you feel or see something, say it!

Start at the bottom, at the stem, and read up to the top; it is quite common to receive strong imprints of the past, especially childhood as this is when the mind was open and we were closest to Spirit.

Remember as with all forms of psychic readings, give everything you receive, the smallest details can often be essential.

Roses, Irises and Carnations are associated with the emotions.

Stalk: Deals with life path, with childhood at the base. You may find marks or discolorations indicating important changes. Smooth bright patches indicating periods of stability.

Take the first third of the flower as the past, the middle third of the flower as the present and the top third of the flower as the next ten years.

Run your fingers over each section pausing at any knots.

Leaves, stalks where smaller separate flowers branch off the main stem, can be seen as present external factors influencing future paths.

For example: Friends, family, work or love affairs.

Buds: Plans in material matters have not yet come to fruition.

Many Leaves: Suggest commitments, friends and family.

Holes in Leaves: Indicate partings that have occurred which are still painful.

A Solitary Bloom: Indicates a person alone either by choice or through necessity.

Discoloration on Stalks and Leaves: Suggests conflicting interests, choices, even opposition.

Flower Rises High Above Leaves and Other Buds: The person may be ambitious and independent.

If Immersed in Foliage Then: Happiness is found through others and through working in caring professions.

Flower Itself: Indicates the person's characteristics both in world and dreams.

Shape is first taken into consideration.

Bloom is Tall and Stately: This denotes a love of travel and restlessness.

A Small and Multi-Petalled Flower: Reflects a love of the familiar and of home. Symmetrical implies a sense of order and a lover of luxury; Oval a degree of self-containment.

Large Rounded Petals: A natural giver, or, with bells on flower, a keeper of secrets.

Tiny Single Flowers: Often means that the inner world and personal happiness are more important than material success.

Main Flower Is Budding: Then it is not yet time for dreams to be fulfilled.

Half-Closed: Suggests hesitance and a lack of confidence.

Open: Means affectionate and generous.

Full-Bloom: Indicates Wisdom.

Fading Bloom: That present life is clouded with regrets.

Look at the Colours nearest to the centre of flower for the true self.

Finally Look at the Colour of the Chosen Flower

Red: Indicates passion and also anger.

Yellow: A desire to be loved and natural optimism.

Blue: A logical but just person.

White: Unworldly and easily hurt.

Pink: Gentle and conciliatory.

Purple: Mysterious and secretive depths.
Brown: Materialistic or practical.
Orange: Confident and independent.
More Than One Colour: Indicates versatility but also changeability.

Face Reading

We all face read and have spent our whole lives studying characters and matching them up with faces. This has been part of our subconscious instinct to protect ourselves. By studying face reading we can turn it into a conscious art and learn how to read faces.

We already intuitively recognize when someone looks to be in poor health. Pale skin, dark bags under the eyes, pale lips, grey skin tones, yellow skin and a yellow hue to the whites of the eyes, a gaunt thin face, spots and pimples will each suggest to us through our natural face reading abilities that the person could be in better health.

As we see faces every day we have a great opportunity to develop our face reading skills, making this art of diagnosis ideal for getting real life experience and practice.

Face reading has been used throughout the Orient as a traditional form of diagnosis. In ancient times physicians' jobs were to help their patients avoid illness and live as long as possible. To do this they needed forms of non-invasive diagnosis that would help them detect when someone was out of balance and at risk of poor health. Facial diagnosis was one way to achieve this. In addition it can be used to read a person's character. Once a reading has been made it is possible to provide advice on diet, lifestyle and natural remedies to help bring the person to a more healthy state of balance.

Face reading can help better our intuition, and by studying our own faces using these face reading techniques we can gather better knowledge of ourselves and others.

I ask my students to each bring a photograph of somebody they know well, either alive or in spirit.

The photographs are then set aside on a table. In turn the photographs will then be picked up and read from. Using focus and intuition, describe any senses, feelings that come to you from observing the photograph.

Face reading is an ancient tradition and the study is fascinating but also extensive. I recommend further reading if you feel drawn to this topic.

Below are a few points to take into consideration while attempting this face reading exercise.

Forehead

The shape of the person's forehead will provide useful clues as to how he or she thinks. A large, high forehead indicates an intelligent and academically active mind. A short forehead suggests quick sharp decision-making. A forehead that is vertical in profile implies independent thinking, making it easier to generate ideas and work alone. A forehead that slopes backwards suggests a more social and interactive disposition. Such a person is excited to express and hear ideas, therefore being a natural team worker.

Eyes

The eyes are said to be the window to the soul. Smaller eyes are a sign of a desire for precision, accuracy and attention to detail as well as being perceptive and able to see through waffling. Larger eyes suggest an open, friendly character that is gentle, kind and accessible. Eyes set close together show great powers of concentration and consistency. Eyes set wide apart are associated with being broadminded and interested in a broader, liberal attitude to life.

Cheeks

Sunken cheeks indicate a serious and responsible attitude to life. Prominent cheeks suggest emotions come up to the surface quickly with a strong desire to express them. Flushed cheeks indicate a state of excitement and a greater desire to speak out. A pale disposition shows a deeper resolve and a drawing in of emotions.

Lips

As lips are a feature that moves they attract attention. Being a point of sexual contact we associate lips with sensuality. Thin lips reflect a hardworking, responsible character that is prone to overworking. Full lips indicate a more relaxed, pleasure orientated nature, knowing how to have fun. A smaller mouth would suggest greater ability to be direct and focus on the job in hand without becoming distracted. A wide mouth shows a desire to take in a broader range of experiences in life and live a more varied and less structured life.

The Envelope Game

The Envelope Game is a little bit like the children's game 'Consequence'; however, the envelope game is a form of psychometry.

For this exercise you will need a large envelope, a piece of paper, a pen or pencil, two or more people and also an intuitive mind.

Write on the paper your name and birth month, a name that is significant to you and a symbol drawing, i.e. a flower or sunshine perhaps. When complete, place the piece of paper inside the envelope.

Place the envelope in your lap or sit on it; if this is comfortable then start the psychic protection exercise and meditation is also recommended.

After the completion of meditation, the envelopes are then

returned to the group leader, who will shuffle them and then hand them out again, one to each person.

The envelopes are now charged with the energy of their owner.

You must now focus your attention on to each envelope that passes you by.

Working clockwise, attempt to write a couple of sentences; the aim is to write down all of your senses, any feelings or vibes you get from each envelope.

Any thoughts, impressions or images, if you sense it, write it.

Do not be afraid, you will be amazed at what you know. Your intuition is that first fleeting glimpse, hint, and knowing. Let it flow, follow it through, believe.

When the last envelope has been completed, the envelopes are then returned to the group leader who will open the envelopes and return each one to its owner.

It is often very rewarding and amusing to read your own envelope, not only to read what your group members have sensed about you, but also to read what you have intuitively sensed about yourself. The results of this exercise have been very rewarding.

Collage Picture Reading

This exercise requires a group effort.

I look forward to this class every time, and I always find the results very rewarding on a deeper level.

The aim of this exercise is to connect with the child within then release it and also form group bonding.

You will need a table (to sit around), magazines, A4 card, glitter/decoration craft items, glue and scissors, and a group of intuitive open–minded participants.

The group will sit around the table after practising the psychic protection exercise. The magazines are there to browse through. I ask the group to cut out any pictures, words, symbols, or colours that they feel drawn to, or feel a particular emotional feeling or vibe about. Using the glue provided create a collage work of pictures, images and words.

It is a really good sound to hear the group getting on with their collage making. Talking about this and that, as they flick through the magazines, new topics come to light. The fun begins and the laughter starts as the pictures start to come together. The sense of free spirit is really felt, as the group really let go of any barriers. Relaxation is achieved at a natural state. The group is bonding and now is subconsciously vibrating at the same level.

At this moment their spiritual bodies are meeting and the energies are passing information via the energy centres, 'the chakras'. The subtle bodies emerge and tell us all we need. It is the mental faculty that interferes with this factor. On a conscious level, it is when we have developed our psychic abilities we can then tap into this well of consciousness.

The pictures and any glitter or decorated objects are glued on to the A4 card to add that personal touch. Using their chosen materials the students make collages that each student feels best represents them, their feelings, emotions and outlook.

On completion of the collages the group must return as a circle. Working clockwise, choose a group member to show their picture to the group.

The other students are to focus on the pictures and the images and draw on any information that is received through the senses, allowing intuition to flow.

The images from the picture act as triggers for the psychic mind.

Working in a group aids learning from each other, group development, progress and self-confidence. I always encourage my group to stand and speak up. I aim to develop self-esteem and confidence.

This group exercise allows others to speak out; sometimes one student may receive impressions that may not have been apparent to another person, but once it has been said they will also connect with the same thing too. Often one student will have lots of things to say while another has been sat quietly and at the end will say, "I was going to say that," or "I was sensing this." If you feel it then say it!

Collage Picture Reading is a very good exercise and always receives very good results. I find that its aid in psychic development is multi-dimensional.

Scrying

Scrying, also known as Crystallomancy, Crystal Gazing and Hydromancy.

The practice of scrying consists of fixing a gaze upon a crystal ball, crystals, precious stones, glass, mirror, water, wax, fire and even smoke.

The practice of scrying stems back into ancient times. It has been reputed that scrying was practised by the Ancient Egyptians who used crystals and precious stones to foretell the future. These scrying crystals were regarded as the 'Eye of Horus'.

In classical Greek mythology three sisters called the Graeae (meaning 'the Old Ones') passed between them one chosen Crystal, giving them second sight. This was said to be a crystal eye, and was borrowed by Perseus as he sought the home of Medusa.

The art of scrying with crystals, stones, water or fire has been practised in one form of another by many worldwide through the Aborigines of Australia, Native American Indians, the Mayans and by the Incas of the South Americas. The ancient Druids are said to have used pyromancy, also a form of scrying, to see future events.

Nostradamus the famous seer and astrologer also used scrying in the aiding of his predictions; it is told that he used water and fire. Nostradamus is said to have predicted such major worldwide events as 'The Great Fire of London', 'The rise of Adolf Hitler' and 'The attack on the World Trade Center'.

After there is great trouble among mankind, a greater one is prepared. The great mover of the universe will renew time, rain, blood, thirst, famine, steel weapons and disease. In the heavens, a fire seen.
– Nostradamus (1503–1566)

The founder and prophet of the Mormon Religion, 'The Church of Jesus Christ and the Latter-day Saints', Joseph Smith, Jr., used a pair of stones described as, "Two smooth three-cornered diamonds". These stones were called 'Urim' and 'Thummim'. These 'seer stones' were used to translate the Book of Mormon from the Golden Plates and other Divine Revelations.

When practising scrying with a crystal ball, crystals, stones, water or fire, or whichever element you feel drawn to, it is important to relax and to keep a clear mind, don't expect anything. It is often the huge expectation that becomes the turn off. Quite often nothing significant happens at all, but over time and with practice our minds become finely tuned instruments. Always keep your diaries close by so you can note anything significant, any experience and progress.

To cleanse crystals and renew energy I advise placing crystals outside over night at the time of the full moon.

Crystals, gem stones, water and any reflective object have a strong affinity with the moon, which is the patron of reflection through its own relationship with the sun. The moon is also emblematic of our emotional, feminine, creative and intuitive side. The moon governs the realm of our dreams and imagi-nation, also ruling the earth's tides and our emotional and receptive states. The human body is made up of around 75% water; as our bodies have a high percentage of fluid we are strongly influenced by the moon. At full moon our feelings become highly sensitized. It is significant to understand that the moon has a powerful, energetic healing effect on crystals.

Crystallomancy

This exercise is based on scrying.

You will need a crystal ball.

This exercise is one that can be practised alone.

Place the crystal on a table in front of you. Many crystal balls you can buy come with their own stand. If you don't have a stand you might like to use a small cushion or a silk handkerchief purchased and reserved especially for this purpose.

Sit down and relax. Lay your hands gently on the ball for a minute or two in order to energize and strengthen your psychic rapport. While holding the crystal ball, consider the purpose of this scrying session. If appropriate try to visualize the subject of your question. Some people like to ask the question out loud, others prefer to meditate on it for a few moments in preparation.

Now, remove your hands from the crystal. Look into the crystal ball. Fix your gaze and allow your eyes to relax and become slightly unfocused.

Don't expect anything. Don't force anything. Just allow yourself to relax and keep gazing upon your crystal ball.

After a little while you may see what appears to be a mist or smoke forming inside the crystal. Let this mist grow and fill the ball, then visualize it gradually clearing to reveal images within the crystal.

The images you see might not be what you expected. That's OK, don't fight them. Your subconscious mind knows what information you need. Just let the images flow, changing and taking you wherever they choose to go. Don't try to rationalize now, time for that later, and just accept whatever you see.

Colours occur frequently along with other symbols.

Once the crystal ball has shown you all the images you need, they will begin to fade.

If your eyes tire and become strained in any way, it is advised to stop this exercise at once.

Below I have added a list of symbols and meanings, although it is a matter for you to use your own intuition when interpreting your visions. How did you feel? Let your senses guide you.

While practising with your crystal ball it is usual to find coloured mist forming, especially in early stages of development. With time and patience your visions will develop into symbolism.

Red: Action, confidence, courage and vitality.

Pink: Love, attraction, emotional well-being and beauty.

Gold: Wealth, prosperity and wisdom.

Yellow: Wisdom, joy, happiness and intellectual energy.

Green: Life, nature, fertility, good health and well-being.

Blue: Youth, spontaneity, spirituality, truth and peace.

Purple: Magic, mystery, secrecy, wisdom and intuition.

White: Purity, cleanliness, spirituality and positivity.

Black or Grey and Dark Mist: Sorrow, sadness, negative energy, aggression and ill health.

Silver: A good outcome, good luck, a positive future, 'Every cloud has a silver lining'.

Cats: Are often a symbol of femininity, feminine influences and intuitiveness.

Dogs: A symbol of loyal friendships.

Bears: A powerful enemy.

Donkey: Hard work is needed, work is starting.

Elephant: Elephants never forget, forgive and let go. The elephants are a symbol of wisdom; they carry a lot of weight and often symbolize the weight one is carrying in a burden of the past.

Tigers and Lions: Can often mean strength of character, or inner strength and endurance is needed.

Fish: Spiritual and religious connections or feelings and emotions.

Frog: Is a symbol of good luck and fortune.

Scorpion: Is an ancient symbol of war. The vision of a scorpion can symbolize trouble in social arenas or within the home.

Spiders: Good fortune, money.

Apple Tree: In mystic literature the Apple Tree is the Tree of Life; to see such a vision indicates good news, new life, gifts, learning and study.

Books: A symbol of learning, knowledge and study.

Candle: A burning candle is a symbol of good health and prosperity, a candle that is dimly lit or extinguished can denote ailing health and ill fortune.

Eggs: A symbol of fertility.

Fire: A symbol of passion, desire and also anger. This symbol forces us to look at our true feelings and emotions; fire spreads and can quickly become out of control if we do nothing.

Flowers: Indicate joy, happiness, beauty, love and romance.

Fruit: Desire, emotional satisfaction, attraction, love, romance, joy and fertility.

Zodiac symbols often draw me to the calendar months and the seasons, i.e. 'the Cancer crab' may intuitively pull me to the month of July and the summertime; therefore I will feel that this month is significant.

Crystal Psychometry

This exercise is based on psychometry and scrying with the use of crystals or crystal pendulums.

Psychometry is often referred to as seeing with the fingers. It's about reading the vibrations of the object by holding them.

Psychometry as a term was coined by Joseph R. Buchanan in 1842. The word stems from psyche and metric, which means 'to measure with the mind'.

Buchanan, an American professor of physiology, was one of the first people to experiment with psychometry. Using his students as subjects, he placed various drugs in glass vials, and then asked the students to identify the drugs merely by holding the vials. Their success rate was more than chance, and he published the results in his book, *Journal of Man*. To explain the phenomenon, Buchanan theorized that all objects have "souls" that retain a memory.

By holding an object in our possession for a while we can charge that object with our own energy and vibration; it is believed that we place an imprint of ourselves upon that object.

You will need assorted crystals or tumble stones, or the students' own crystal pendulums, a bag (pouch) and two or more persons.

Place a set amount of crystals (equal to the amount in the group) in a bag. Allow each person to take a crystal at random from the bag.

Practise the psychic protection ritual followed by meditation. While in meditation keep the crystal in your hand.

After meditation place all crystals back in the bag. Shuffle them up and in turn each group member will take one crystal at random.

If using your own crystal pendulums, students are to place them into the pouch after the ritual and meditation and continue as with crystals or stones.

With crystal in hand the aim is to use your senses to feel any vibrations left on the crystal from its keeper.

Each person must attempt to stand and speak out about any feelings and senses that they draw from the crystal in hand.

Clairsentience really comes into effect here. How do you feel? Notice any emotional shifts. Sometimes we don't realize small changes, such as we may start scratching our skin. Why? Were we itchy before the exercise? Is this somebody with a skin condition or allergy? We suddenly feel emotional, a little sad, or upset. Why? Is the focus on the emotional well-being here? We must realize these subtle shifts in our feelings and senses and relate them to the recipient.

This exercise is a good form of psychometry. It is very good focus for intuition and practising psychic development.

It is said that we are drawn to the crystals that we come into contact with. Crystals hold a lot of energy and assist with energy flow. Crystals are renowned for their therapeutic and healing benefits. It is said that when we are drawn to a crystal it is because we are drawn to the healing energy of that crystal.

When using crystals and crystal pendulums with this practical exercise it is worth taking into consideration the crystal itself and the benefits that it carries. It may be a pointer that the person it is connected with requires the energy and assistance of that particular crystal. The crystal itself may in fact give a pointer and clue to the personality of whom it belongs.

For Example: **Amber** – Stimulates the intellect; assists in releasing the old and embracing the new.

A person who is drawn to Amber, I find, will have self-esteem issues relating to the past. People who are drawn to Amber usually find themselves talking about and reliving the past.

Other Crystals and their healing properties

Amethyst: Calms the mind, treats insomnia and brings restful sleep. Amethyst has strong healing and cleansing powers, and enhances spiritual awareness.

Bloodstone: Gives courage, an excellent grounding and protection stone. It heightens intuition and increases creativity.

Carnelian: Promotes positivity and banishes emotional negativity. It gives courage and dispels apathy, motivates success. Carnelian is useful for overcoming abuse of any kind.

Citrine: Raises self-esteem and self-confidence, it enhances individuality, improves motivation, activates creativity and encourages self-expression. This encouraging stone helps with concentration and verbalizing thoughts and feelings.

Clear Quartz: Aids concentration and unlocks memory, enhances psychic awareness and raises energy levels.

Jade: Signifies wisdom and harmony, a protective stone, increases love and nurturing. It is believed to attract good luck and friendship.

Lapis Lazuli: Stimulates enlightenment and psychic ability. This stone brings balance to the mind, body and spirit, promoting deep inner knowledge and encourages self-awareness.

Rose Quartz: Is the crystal of heart, bringing healing, calm and peace, attracting love, and promotes self-love. Restoring trust and harmony, encourages self-forgiveness and acceptance.

Tigers Eye: Is a protective stone and traditionally was carried as a talisman against ill wishing and curses. It assists in accomplishing goals, self-realization and promotes clarity of intention.

Turquoise: Brings balance and calm, it strengthens and stabilizes mood swings. It stimulates romantic love. Turquoise is an excellent stone for exhaustion, depression and anxiety

Crystal Psychometry – One to One

You will need a pouch of crystals, I recommend using 12 crystals or tumble stones. This exercise is based on crystal psychometry explained previously. Although in this instance we are to work in pairs on a one to one basis.

Take your pouch of crystals, and after you have followed your psychic protection ritual open yourself to read for your sitter.

Ask your sitter to choose a number between 1 and 12 (the number of stones present inside of your pouch). You can then pass your pouch of crystals to the sitter to take the amount of stones chosen, after which he/she will pass back to you, the reader.

Sit with the crystals, either in your hand or place them on the table. With practice you will become more and more in tune with your crystals. Allow their colours, their shapes, their flaws and their attributes to influence your reading. Most of all allow your intuitive mind to flow, learn how to be in touch with your senses and feelings.

After much practice you will come to realize your readings becoming more accurate, and the crystals are but a focus for your psychic mind.

Pyromancy

Due to the importance of fire in society from the earliest of times, it is quite likely that pyromancy was one of the earlier forms of divination. It is said that in Greek society virgins at the Temple of Athena in Athens regularly practised pyromancy. It is also possible that followers of Hephaestus, the Greek god of fire, practised pyromancy. In ancient China, pyromancy was practised in the form of burning or heating oracle bones, usually the scapulae (shoulder blades) of oxen or turtle shells, to produce cracks which were then read as portents.

One of the first oracles to take advantage of the mind's ability to form pictures from random shapes was pyromancy, the art of divination from fire. It is thought that this divination technique may have originated from the times when burnt offerings were made to the gods. The ancient seers would study the flames as the sacrifices were made and from them interpret the images.

Visual projection techniques were used by the shaman seers as a means of stimulating clairvoyance and knowledge of the future.

The technique involves sitting quietly in front of a fire and entering a relaxed state. Salt, leaves or other objects of sacrifice can be placed beforehand; the object is to detach your mind and allow yourself to see like the ancient pyromancers.

This ancient technique can produce surprising results. Sit before a roaring fire and ask your question. Gaze into the flames while the fire burns down. If it is not possible to light a fire, then pyromancy can be achieved using a candle.

Within the flames, or in the sparkling, glowing coals below them, images of the future may appear. Interpret them with symbolic thought. It's best to limit gazing time to about 10–20 minutes, but there's no need to check your watch. Allow the images to come to you for an appropriate time. A number of different pictures may appear but one should stand out from the rest as being particularly significant, then this is considered to be important and is interpreted as the oracle for the future.

Once the symbol from the fire has been determined, it is inter-preted according to a set of traditional meanings. For example, a windmill will represent a change for the better, as will a fountain and a wheel.

In Sacrificial Pyromancy, it was said that the future was bright and good when the flames burned profusely, and when produced a roaring fire for length then the future was full of success, work and activity, a good harvest! When the fire fizzled and was slow burning, this foretold of a bad omen, perhaps drought and famine!

Whatever you feel, sense or see you must always remain faithful to your intuition, because it is intuition that is the key to pyromancy.

For symbols see also *Scrying*.

Colour Cards

This exercise is similar to working with Zener Cards. Zener Cards were produced in 1930 by Joseph Rhine and Karl Zener to measure ESP and in particular telepathy.

A pack of Zener Cards consists of 25 cards of different symbols: a Black Square, Green Star, Red Cross, Orange Circle and Blue Wavy Lines. The cards would be shuffled and the 'sender' would concentrate on each card, and by telepathy from the mind send the image of each card to the 'receiver', who would be seated in another room, or in another building.

This experiment would be repeated again and again, to reduce the possibility of chance affecting the outcome. The results achieved were startling.

To use colour cards will require you to make your very own.

You will need card, scissors and colouring pencils, crayons or markers.

Cut out 25 pieces. I recommend the size of each card to be 2" x 3".

Choose 5 colours to use and divide your set of colour cards into five. I recommend colouring 5 red, 5 yellow, 5 blue, 5 orange and 5 green. You can differ from this, or in time produce more colour cards and combine them.

Once you have made your own set of colour cards you are ready to start. These colour cards are now personal to you and are charged with your energy; make sure that the energy that you have charged them with is positive. Positive intentions are required in the making of your colour cards.

Take care of your cards, maybe keep them in a handkerchief or box.

Colour cards are used as a focus for the mind; they are a tool to sharpen your intuition and psychic impressions.

When you are ready shuffle your colour cards.

When working alone, take one card at a time and lay it face down on a table. Hold your hand over or touch the card.

Receive the impression from the card. Don't try to determine what the colour of the card is. Allow the impression of the card to come to you.

This exercise is a focus for your mind; it is a tool to sharpen your intuition and psychic impressions.

If the card is a red card, you may see images of fire, or blood, you may see danger flash in your mind. You may receive the clairsentient impression of warmth or receive a hot flush.

If the card is blue you may feel cold. You may see images of the sky or the sea.

If the card is orange you may feel a sensation of being warm, you may smell or even taste oranges in your mouth. You may see the images of oranges, see the sunshine, you may feel a sense of vibrancy and radiance.

You may receive the impressions of Oranges, smelling or tasting them if the Colour Card is Orange.

With each card your intuition will tell you what the colour is on the opposite side of each card. Allow your instincts and feelings to guide you.

When working in pairs: You will need a notebook and pen, one set of colour cards and two people.

One person is to be the 'Sender' and the other will be the 'Receiver'.

The sender will shuffle the cards and cut the pack in half. It is recommended to set the cards down on a table, and then take one card at a time.

Take the top card, each turn, and focus your attention on that card for three minutes. When the sender has finished they can clap their hands or ring a bell so that the receiver knows another image is about to be transmitted.

The receiver is to focus for yet another three minutes, either in another room or in the same room, and make a note of what colour impression comes to him/her.

When the sender has transmitted half of the pack, take a short break and then change over.

You may find that you are astounded by the results that you achieve. Don't be disheartened if you find you don't excel your own expectations. Practice will only improve your psychic awareness.

Automatic Writing

While writing *The 5 Points of Power and Wisdom*, I took dictation and guidance using automatic writing and channelling.

Automatic writing is the process or method of writing material that does not come from the conscious or deliberate thoughts of the writer. The writer's hand forms the message, and the person is unaware of what will be written. This form of writing is often performed while in a trance state. Other times the writer is aware of his or her immediate surroundings but not of the actions of their writing hand or the messages being written.

Automatic writing is often used by spiritualists as a form of psychic channelling.

Automatic writing is essentially writing that is done in an altered state of consciousness that is attributed to spirits of the dead. It is believed by some that the spirits literally manipulate the writing utensil in the hands of the medium to communicate. The writer is often unaware of what is being written and often even scrawls out text in handwriting that is markedly different than his own. Others believe that perhaps the spirits may also communicate by forming messages in the mind of the medium, which reproduce on the page. Most likely though, the medium is writing unconsciously and messages are formed from material in the subconscious mind or from a secondary personality that is gifted with extrasensory perception. This same explanation may apply to messages received by Ouija boards as well.

The notion of subconscious communication was popular with many well-known modern artists and was used as a method for creating original artwork. Artists such as Jackson Pollock and Salvador Dali utilized automatic painting techniques in their works.

The impressions received through automatic channelling can be in the form of pictures, i.e. psychic art, words, poetry, lyrics and numbers. The words can be mirror images, written backwards, even sometimes starting from the bottom of the page up to the top.

I have used automatic writing or automatic channelling with written work, including poetry and also with my other visual artwork, which is included in my art exhibitions and my book of poetry – *Dreams Unwind*.

Steps for Automatic Writing

- Ground and Protect yourself using the techniques described in the chapter **Psychic Protection**.
- Call upon your Spirit Guides to be present and guide you within your practice.
- Sit comfortably and relax.
- Provide yourself with a pen or pencil and paper to write with.
- Close your eyes and take deep breaths... Relax.
- State a clear question; maybe ask for guidance or direction.
- When you feel ready, let go and begin to write. Allow any information to flow freely on to the paper.
- You may feel that your arm tingles, or a sense of pressure, heaviness in your arm or a vibration shift.
- Your hand may start to automatically move by itself, or you may find information forming in your mind as thoughts that you feel utterly inspired and compelled to put on to the paper.
- Words, number, pictures, allow the vibe to flow through you.
- Do not judge or analyse – just let the messages gently stream on to the paper. Keep a clear and open mind.
- For your first time, allow about 10–15 minutes and then continue however long you feel the messages coming.
- You will know when you are finished!
- Thank your source and come back into the room.

Love is Power

I was given dictation through Automatic Writing/Channelling. I have looked at this process further in the chapter **Methods for Psychic Development**. I channelled this automatic dictation from my Spirit Guide, 'Charles'. This guidance came at different times and at different intervals, the writing was varied, at times the writing was very clear, and at other times it was difficult to read. I have to remark that the writing differed from my own. This is what was channelled to me:

Love is power and light.

Without love there is nothing. Nothingness is chaos.

Love is eternal.

Nothingness is darkness.

Cast out the shadows from your mind, don't look back is to forgive, disengage, detach the mind from the dark.

The 5 Points of power and wisdom are Love, Gratitude, Confidence, Belief and Forgiveness.

The Holy and the Divine rituals are within you keeping you home. Walk with us to the Divine Temple, you will be successful on your journey. *** Light and Wisdom to All –

The light of the soul burns bright, truth is your guide.

Love is beauty and beauty is within, Ask and we will show you yours –

Oh Divine Beauty how you shine, the sparks of beauty cascade from you. **

Forgive. Forgive my everything. My All.

The fountain of youth calls, wash away the pain of yesterday and bathe in the waters of youthful exile, in the glory of innocence, and innocent laughter, carefree like children.

Disengage the mind from all that's gone before, there is no past, no future, only today. Time is an illusion. We correct our thoughts today create and illuminate our path with love and peace.

I shall tell you more;

In my journey, I was given complete notice of my surroundings.

I come to you with my intentions;

You my dear are of distinction and of purpose.

My intentions are to love, to protect, to guide, Also to Teach.

I give blessings to you, let me start.

My name is Charles;

The 5 points of power and wisdom should be very clear and very profound.

To start; the love of the Divine holds no Boundaries. The divine wisdom is a multi layer dimension and is effortless.

Love is an unfolding reality, essential to every human beings development on the earth, essential to the evolution standing *

Without Love, there simply isn't life.

The Divine presence himself is love.

Love is the truth of all matter.

To be within Love is to be happy, and happiness is the gift of God.

God creates love in this world and asks that all of his creations find comfort within his Kingdom.

Love is the Kingdom, Love is Home, Happiness is Bliss, Joy is the union. To be anywhere other is to live separated from a Divine inspired life.

Remember with every decision that you make the feeling of bliss tells you that you're home.

*(To) live without worry, cast all doubts out of your minds. To Trust and have faith is to place all of the earthly ** (Cares and worries) into the hands of god.

Taking that leap of faith is often hard for those attached with material wealth and benefits of the earth.

To place all faith and trust into the hands of the provider, into the hands of the Divine, is to ask that all will be provided, all cares are taken, all worries are taken, to trust you are safe, and never hunger.

To trust is to have a life of abundance. *(As) faith occurs one can walk the path of a free and righteous man, living in light, living in love, living a creative life full of * (abundance). For those who gave up attachment, Faith is the Key.

To this life of non attachment, Ask and ye shall receive – * Belief. Spiritual wealth.

I will give you all; we take nothing except for your promise of Love.

All that God asks of us, is that we Love and allow ourselves to be loved in return.

* Unreadable dictation.

Guided Meditation – The Secret Garden

- Always wear loose fitting clothes for comfort and please make sure that you have visited the toilet beforehand. The aim is to rid yourself of as many distractions as possible.
- Focus on your grounding and psychic protection exercise beforehand.
- Start the meditation by playing some gentle, relaxing music. Now lay or sit comfortably, hands at your side or in your lap.
- Once you have accomplished a comfortable sitting or lying position, take three cleansing deep breaths.
- With each breath allow yourself to deeply relax.
- There is nothing you must do now, you are allowing yourself 15–20 minutes relaxation and this is OK. There is nothing to tend to, let go of the day, it is your time now.
- Relax deeply... breathe in and out at a comfortable and relaxed pace; allow your breathing to relax you further.
- Relax your arms, relax your legs, and relax your shoulders.
- If you find yourself losing focus, focus once again on your breathing and relax your shoulders.
- Focus your attention on the door in your mind; when ready, walk through this...
- Stepping out on to a path, walk down the gravel path to a gate, open the gate and walk through the gate.
- You are now stood inside a beautiful garden, a secret garden... Allow your mind now to explore the garden, what's inside your garden? Wild flowers, a lake, a stream, a pond with fish, butterflies or birds? Is your garden enclosed? Maybe your garden is surrounded by a wall or is it free and endless?
- Allow yourself to roam here for a while in this secret garden, feeling relaxed and free.

- The sun is out and there is a warm feeling here. The sunlight shines through the trees and as you gently tread with bare feet you feel a connection with the earth and the universe.
- You see a bench and are drawn to sit here.
- Does anyone join you here? Maybe a Spirit Guide, an Angel Guide, or the spirit of a loved one will come and sit with you. This is your time, don't question, just accept what comes to your mind, maybe you are left a gift on the bench? Something that helps answer a question to a problem in life?
- When you feel your time here has come to an end, walk back to your gate, walk through it, and close it behind you. Walk back up the path and back through your door. Remember to close your door.
- This meditation has brought many good results and is indeed one of my personal and also teaching favourites.
- Remember to always close down using the techniques from psychic protection; don't leave yourself vulnerable to negative energies that exist in the world.

Log your experiences in your spiritual diary.

Guided Meditation – The Crystal Cave

- I often choose to practise this meditation using my crystal pendulum or a favourite energizing crystal such as clear quartz known for its use in aiding psychic attunement. I often find that it helps restore my energy, and aids with my vision.
- Always wear loose fitting clothes for comfort and please make sure that you've visited the toilet beforehand. The aim is to rid yourself of as many distractions as possible.
- Focus on your grounding and psychic protection exercise beforehand.
- Start the meditation by playing some gentle and relaxing music. Now lay or sit comfortably, hands at your side or in your lap.
- Once you have accomplished a comfortable sitting or lying position, take three cleansing deep breaths.
- With each breath allow yourself to deeply relax.
- There is nothing you must do now, you are allowing yourself 15–20 minutes relaxation and this is OK. There is nothing to tend to, let go of the day, it is your time now.
- Relax deeply... breathe in and out at a comfortable and relaxed pace; allow your breathing to relax you further.
- Relax your arms, relax your legs, relax your shoulders, relax your hands and relax your feet down to your toes. Deeply relax allowing yourself to let go into a comfortable state of calm and relaxation.
- If you find yourself losing focus, focus once again on your breathing and relax your shoulders.
- Focus your attention on the door in your mind; when ready, walk through this...
- Stepping out on to a path, walk down the gravel path to a gate, open the gate and walk through it.

- Once out of the gate you look down to notice you have stepped on to a path of crystals. You feel compelled to walk along this path.
- This path of crystals feels energized, and you feel a positive vibration from the many different coloured crystals.
- You feel vibrant, radiant and energetic, and almost feel as if you wish to skip along this path.
- You notice in the distance a mound of crystals, bigger than you have ever seen; the energy pulls you in.
- On approach you can see a crystal cave.
- The lights seem to shine, shimmer and reflect from the many crystals that are gathered here; you are drawn inside the cave.
- The feeling is light, warm, energetic, and you feel an instant healing energy inside here.
- Within the centre of the cave you notice a huge clear crystal, a diamond or quartz; you feel drawn to the crystal's amazing energy and power.
- Take a moment to visualize your surroundings, take in the energy and healing power within this mystical crystal cave.
- Find yourself standing in the centre of the cave with your hands on the huge powerful clear crystal. As you stand here connected with this awesome crystal you can feel the energy begin to energize you; you feel a strong connection and feel cleansed and healed by the properties of this crystal.
- (Within meditation the crystal inside the crystal cave may differ if we are in need of the properties from other crystals: i.e. amethyst helps brings balance and calm to the mind and promotes good healthy sleep.)
- As you gaze upon this amazing crystal, images and symbols begin to develop, you may experience feelings

and sensations. You may feel that you are drawn into the crystal and your mind begins to wander. Allow your mind to become deeper entranced by the crystal; allow this magical journey to bring a wealth of enlightenment.

- Take your time here and allow feelings and images to wash over you.
- Who do you meet? What do you see? What do you feel? What do you sense?
- Don't question your experience; just allow the experience to happen. Relax and breathe.
- When you feel you are complete in your journey make your way back to the crystal path, back though the gate and back through your door.
- Always close your door on return. Practise the closing down and psychic protection exercise as provided.
- After meditation it is recommended to take a drink, clap your hands, and place yourself firmly back into the earth plane once again.

Remember to write down your journey in your spiritual diary.

Guided Meditation – Opening of the Third Eye

Always practise the grounding and psychic protection exercise before starting meditation.

I recommend wearing loose fitting clothing for comfort and relaxation purposes. The playing of soothing music is also recommended to enhance and deepen the meditative state.

- Sit or lay down in a comfortable position.
- Take deep breaths and allow yourself to relax deeply.
- Let go of the events of the day, remind yourself this is your time, and everything is OK.
- Relax with every breath that you take. Relax your arms, relax your legs and relax your shoulders. Allow yourself to slumber into a deep relaxation.
- The focus is on the opening of the chakras. Starting at the Base Chakra focus all of your attention here.
- Working your way up through your chakra you will see your chakras as they are, colourful and glowing with energy. The more you focus on your chakra centre the more vibrant and active they seem to become.
- When you come to your Brow Chakra, rest here and focus all of your attention on this chakra. Look at the colour, vibrancy, the radiance, and the energy. When you feel you have truly opened this chakra and you have focused your attention here, feel your focus being pulled to your forehead.
- Your attention will now rest in between your eyebrows. You will feel a tingling here, a tickle or other sensation as you sense a slight vibration or energy shift. You have now stimulated the pineal gland by using your focus and intention.

- With your intention, will your mind's eye to open; it may be instantaneous or it may take a while. Stay relaxed and stay focused on your breathing.
- When your third eye opens look at her beauty. What colour is your eye? How do you feel? What do you see? What are your emotions? How does it appear? Take in everything; let it all come to you.
- Take some time to focus on your third eye; as you look into your mind's eye you will receive a vision, an image that has meaning for you or lesson to be learned, a vision for the future or a message from your higher self.

If you don't find you achieve instant results then try again. Never give up!

Forever Mindful

It is very important to generate a good attitude, a good heart, as much as possible. From this, happiness in both the short term and the long term for both yourself and others will come.
– Dalai Lama

We are here as bright open channels ready to connect. Often viewed as an exciting quest, and to those who are in the dark, psychic work can be viewed as an easy position to take, 'Easy money or an easy life'.

I am sure there are those out there who are out to make a quick buck, and have little spiritual interest in their working practice. I believe the laws of cause and effect, 'karma' will deal with this. "What goes around comes around."

My belief system is essential to my working practice. I do believe that I am looked after, *everything happens for a reason*, I am sent what I need on a daily basis, and there is always a reason and always a purpose for each encounter. There are no coincidences. I am here to learn and also to teach, and to reach personal enlightenment.

On the contrary my work is not easy; if I viewed it as a quick buck and had no conscience then yes, but I believe I was chosen for this lifestyle, it is a part of me and I am a part of it.

Each time I am sent a sitter, I must be mindful of their feelings, of their place and situation in life. I realize that this person in front me has been sent to me for a reason, the message may be so small and so insignificant to me, but everything that I channel I have to trust, I have to believe in and I have to maintain that confidence in myself that what I am giving is in truth, light and love. I must remain empathic, caring and non-judgmental despite my sitter's problems or challenges. It is not for us to judge!

I must communicate openly, honestly, but remaining mindful of their current feelings, whether they're grieving, and have emotional issues and want love and relationship advice or financial and career guidance. Sometimes the situation may appear to be trivial, but they are very, very important life issues to the sitter.

When we sense, feel and see events in our sitter's life that warn us of danger, hazards, upsets and illness, it is only with time and with practice that we will know the words to choose and the approach to take. Finding words of comfort and support comes with time.

It is important to have a good attitude towards your life and working practice. The 5 Points of Power and Wisdom provide this basis and will help to build a solid and healthy foundation for the future.

I maintain a healthy and positive outlook about myself and others by maintaining balance and focus.

Love, I love myself and accept myself because I have found and uncovered the inner me, the real self. Through this discovery I have found I am much more understanding of others, more patient, caring, empathic, kind and loving. Through love I have found peace. We are all one and we all connect on a universal consciousness, the collective conscious, one love.

Belief, I have unwavering belief, faith and trust. Without that belief my connection with my Spirit and Angel Guides wouldn't be so strong. Through Belief I have established a firm connection, I am a bright channel and through this I can successfully channel accurate help and spiritual guidance into many people's lives.

Gratitude, I am so grateful for all that I have and all that I am and for all that I can be. I am thankful for every experience and every hurdle that I have climbed. I see every obstacle as a valuable lesson that has only made me wiser and stronger and I am truly thankful. I wouldn't change who I am. I know that by being grateful for every blessing that comes to me there are more blessings waiting to grace me.

Forgiveness seems to be at times the most important lesson that I have had to learn and sometimes it seems maybe the lesson in life that I had more to benefit from. Before I forgave all of my grievances, the pain and the pent up anger that I was hoarding, my life was pretty much a mess. I wasn't going anywhere. It would seem that as soon as I forgave those in my past and also myself I could look forward into the future. For the first time it would seem I could move on with my life, and see the future as something positive.

Self-Confidence took a long time for me to gain. My life has seen much destruction and degradation and my self-worth had certainly taken a beating. Using such mind tools as positive thinking, affirmations, and positive visualization really helped. Setting realistic goals and making notes of my achievements. Through meditation and coming into contact with my Spirit Guides and Guardian Angels, also finding and revealing my true-self helped to gain a positive state of mind that really helped manifest my self-esteem and self-image.

The 5 Points of Power and Wisdom is an essential philosophy and I feel that they will help bring personal power, inspiration and a positive outlook to anyone who follows the course and the exercises outlined. After all they have made a major impact on my life.

A good heart is better than all the heads in the world.
– Proverb

We are blessed with wisdom and guidance from a divine energy, within truth and light we are able to assist people in their lives helping them gain a better perspective.

If my belief was not strong, then I would not be a psychic.

Belief and self-confidence are vital components of our recognition in psychic development. The messages that you channel you must believe have been given for a purpose and that they are necessary for the sitter at this point in their lives. Like sowing seeds, they need time to grow. The sitter may have come with another agenda, but then leave with something unexpected.

I believe that every message which I am given is for healing purposes.

We cannot always tell a person what they want to hear, and sometimes a sitter may dismiss facts due to embarrassment, secrecy or denial, or through lack of remembering. We must learn to give information we channel with confidence, knowing that it will help change the sitter's future to bring about a positive outcome.

We must remember we cannot help everyone! Our will may be strong; all we can ever do is to have good intentions. We must realize that once we have given the information in a positive, caring light, we cannot be responsible for that person and how they choose to live their lives. We are only a channel for those seeking guidance. We have to have faith that the guidance we have given will have a positive impact. We all have free will.

We cannot change other people; we can only ever change ourselves.
– Nicola Jayne

Recommended Reading

The following books that I have listed here I personally recommend for reading. I have read these books myself and feel these books have added enormously to my knowledge and personal progress.

A Course in Miracles, Foundation for inner peace. Viking, 1975

Gifts from A Course in Miracles, Frances Vaughan and Roger Walsh. Tarcher/Penguin, 1983

A Return to Love: Reflections on the Principles of a "Course in Miracles", Marianne Williamson. Thorsons/Harper Collins, 1992

The Holy Bible

The Science of Mind, Ernest Holmes. Tarcher/Penguin, 1938

The Secret Teachings of All Ages, Manly P. Hall. Tarcher/Penguin, 1928

A Guide for the Advanced Soul, Susan Hayward. Hayward Books, 1984

Sefer Yetzirah: The Book of Creation, Revised by Rabbi Aryeh Kaplan. Weiser Books

The Essence of Kabbalah, Brian L. Lancaster. Eagle Editions, 2006

The Complete Kabbalah Course, Paul Roland. Quantum, 2005

A Garden of Pomegranates: Skrying on the Tree of Life, Israel Regardie. Llewellyn

The Tree of Life: An Illustrated Study in Magic, Israel Regardie. Llewellyn

At the Feet of The Master, Jiddu Krishnamurti. The Theosophical Press

Total Freedom, Jiddu Krishnamurti. HarperCollins

The Light of the Soul, Alice A. Bailey. Lucis Publishing, 1927

Shamanism: a Beginners Guide, Teresa Moorey. Hodder and Stoughton, 1997

The World of Shamanism, Roger Walsh, MD Ph.D. Llewellyn, 2007

The Lightworker's Way, Doreen Virtue. Hay House

Healing with the Angels, Doreen Virtue. Hay House

Alchemical Healing, Nicki Scully. Bear & Company, 2007

The Book of Alchemy, Francis Melville. Fair Winds Press

The Secret, Rhonda Byrne. Simon & Schuster, 2006

The Book of Secrets, Deepak Chopra. Rider, 2004

The Love Poems of Rumi, Edited by Deepak Chopra. Harmony 1998

The Ultimate Encyclopaedia of Mythology, Arthur Cotterell & Rachel Storm. Hermes House, 1999

The Crystal Bible, Judy Hall. Godsfield Press, 2003

The Astrology Bible, Judy Hall. Godsfield Press, 2005

A Complete Guide to Psychic Development, Cassandra Eason. Piatkus, 1997

The Psychic Handbook; Craig and Jane Hamilton-Parker. Vermilion, 1995

The Psychic Workshop, Kim Chestney. Adams Media, 2004

BOOKS

6th Books investigates the paranormal, supernatural, explainable or unexplainable. Titles cover everything included within parapsychology: how to, lifestyles, beliefs, myths, theories and memoir.